G000123850

TRAVELS
in My Eighties

TRAVELS
in My Eighties

An Account of Twelve Travels Abroad
during the Years of 2009-2012

DERMOT HOPE-SIMPSON

authorHOUSE®

AuthorHouse™ UK Ltd.
1663 Liberty Drive
Bloomington, IN 47403 USA
www.authorhouse.co.uk
Phone: 0800.197.4150

Published by AuthorHouse 07/29/2014

ISBN: 978-1-4969-8332-9 (sc)
ISBN: 978-1-4969-8333-6 (e)

This book is dedicated to my late wife, Jacynth,
with whom I spent so much time travelling.

My thanks are also due to the following individuals and groups:

Anne and Alan Dollery of Kingswood Books, without whose help and encouragement this volume would never have seen the light of day.

My daughter, Elinor, who has always encouraged me to continue with my journeys.

The staff of the Sherborne branch of Bath Travel, who have spent so much time discovering the travel agents who were able to satisfy my requirements.

Those agents, listed in alphabetical order, who made the arrangements for these various journeys: Anatolian Sky, Cox & Kings, Eastern Approaches, Kirker, Regent, and Saga.

The many guides and drivers who have cheerfully put up with my requests.

Most of all, I would like to thank the citizens of the many countries I have visited who, regardless of the views of their respective governments or religions, welcomed me as a guest with such cheerful hospitality.

In the Siq, Petra, Jordan.

CONTENTS

Introduction ix

Chapter 1.   Albania: The Land of the Mercedes Cars 1
Chapter 2.   Istanbul: A City on Two Continents... 26
Chapter 3.   Jordan: A Country of Contrasts 42
Chapter 4.   Uzbekistan and the Golden Road to Samarkand 58
Chapter 5.   Northeast Turkey: Trabzon to Erzurum 77
Chapter 6.   Warsaw and the Chopin Anniversary 97
Chapter 7.   Iran: Land of the Ayatollah 107
Chapter 8.   Southeast Turkey: The Cradle of Civilisation 130
Chapter 9.   Georgia: A Former Russian Republic Full of Active Churches 153
Chapter 10.   Inland Illyria: Kosovo and Northern Albania 183
Chapter 11.   Armenia and Nagorno Karabagh 203
Chapter 12.   Istanbul and Central Anatolia.. 231

Addenda... 255
About the Author 257
About the Book.. 259

Travels in My Eighties

Statue of King Timur, Samarkand, Uzbekistan.

INTRODUCTION

When my wife, Jacynth, died in July 2008, I was seventy-nine years old. We had been married for nearly fifty-three years, and it was obvious that my whole way of life would change. I determined that I would remain active as long as possible and immediately set about looking at the different ways in which I could occupy myself.

I started by becoming a room guide, for one day a week, at Montacute House, a lovely National Trust property in Somerset, UK, near Yeovil. I busied myself in church matters and soon found myself a member of our Diocesan Synod and then of the Diocesan Board of Education. I also became a member of the Standing Committee of our Deanery Synod. But above all, I determined to continue to travel abroad.

Due to the Second World War, I had not travelled abroad until after I had just left school and before my National Service, when an aunt took me to Ascona in Switzerland on Lake Majiore. As an undergraduate at Oxford, a college friend and I hitchhiked round France, and later I took a skiing holiday with the rest of my family at Lech in Austria. Otherwise, apart from several trips to Ireland, which I hardly count as going abroad, I did no more travelling until our honeymoon in 1955, and it was this trip which gave both Jacynth and me a real love of travelling.

It was well before the time that air travel for holidays became the norm, and so we travelled by train to Rijeka, on the Adriatic, with the customary stop at Basle, in Switzerland, for a breakfast of croissants and black cherry jam. We then travelled by boat down the coast of what was then Yugoslavia (there was no proper coastal road), stopping off for two nights at Split and then on past Hvar and Korcula to Dubrovnik, where we spent a few days.

Dubrovnik, Croatia.

Mostar, Bosnia.

We next travelled by a wood-burning train, via Mostar, to Sarajevo, where we changed onto a more modern form of rail transport to get to Belgrade. We arrived starving, since the promised restaurant car had not arrived, and we had only eaten a few lumps of sugar soaked in the local plum brandy since breakfast twenty-four hours before. We were greeted at our hotel with tall glasses each containing two raw eggs, which went down a treat.

After our stop at Belgrade, we were due to travel to Athens. Unfortunately, the train was so crowded that we literally could not squeeze onto it, and our pre-booked sleepers were not due to be attached till shortly before the Greek frontier. When the next train, much slower though labelled the Tauern Express, arrived, the authorities, who felt they had lost face, turned some of their own unfortunate citizens out of their compartment for us. One must remember that tourists there were still rare; indeed, there were only about five thousand British visitors to Yugoslavia that year.

An hour before we reached the Greek frontier, all the lights in the train were switched off, and armed police with powerful torches entered our compartment several times, searching under the seats and on the luggage racks to make sure we were not trying to hide anyone wishing to escape the country. As a result of our late arrival, we only had one full day in Athens before taking a boat to Naples, due to travel through the Corinth Canal. However, naval manoeuvres meant that the canal was closed, and we had to sail right round the Peloponnese, arriving in Naples just in time to catch the last train to Rome, so we were not able to make our planned trip to Pompeii. After two days in Rome, we returned by train back to England.

Despite, or even because of, our difficulties, we both decided that travel was for us, when finances permitted.

The next year, we accompanied Jacynth's parents on a trip to the Baltic states in their Dormobile. Since this was in the days before roll-on and roll-off ferries, we several times had the sight of our vehicle being loaded or unloaded by crane, a long and rather hazardous-looking procedure.

The airplane was to make travelling a lot easier. Our first air tour was in the early 1960s, and it really was an air tour, for all our travelling was in the same ancient plane, with its crew, for the whole of the trip. We flew first to Athens, with refuelling stops at Nice and Brindisi. After a few days, we moved on for three nights in Rhodes and then three more nights in Crete, which still only had a very few made-up roads outside the capital. We finally spent two nights in Rome, with only one refuelling stop required from there on our way back to England.

During our married life, we visited most of the countries in the European Union as well as Yugoslavia, Armenia, Georgia, Lebanon, Syria, Libya, Tunisia, Morocco, and Cyprus. Turkey became our great stamping ground.

Sbeitla, Tunisia.

Salt Lake, near Larnaca, Cyprus.

We soon discovered the advantages of Fly-drive and only took tours when it seemed too difficult to do it in any other way, such as in Libya and Uzbekistan. We also visited places before they were discovered by the tourist hordes. For instance, the first time we were in Ephesus, we were the only two visitors there for some three hours, and even then, it never became really crowded. Many of the places we visited have few foreigners visiting them even today. On one occasion, when we spent three weeks in eastern Turkey, we only met one English person after leaving the airport. In a pair of extraordinary coincidences, we discovered that my uncle had been her doctor when she was a child, and I had recently been teaching her nephew and niece. We did have other coincidences happen while travelling. One day, we ran into our next-door neighbours from Plymouth, and none of us had realised the others were going to Greece, while even odder was the time we saw the same married couple on three holidays in succession in three different countries and at three different times of year.

But now I was on my own, and the question arose as to where and by what means I should travel. The where was soon decided. For most of our married life, Albania had been a closed and mysterious land under the dictatorship of Hoxha. We had travelled all round the frontier at different times. Indeed, I was once nearly arrested for taking an illegal photograph across the border. I knew quite a bit about the history of the country for we had collected old, mainly nineteenth-century books about Turkey in Europe, and of course Albania was featured in them. Even when the country had opened itself up to tourists after the death of Hoxha, the infrastructure was still very poor, and we had to content ourselves with a day trip from neighbouring Corfu to Saranda to see the Roman site of Butrint. The road from Saranda to Butrint was in such a state that we decided it was not yet the time to make a longer visit. However, the country had always beckoned me, and I now determined to go. I did not wish to travel entirely by myself, so I booked for one of the few tours available, leaving in the spring of 2009.

The mosque in Tirana, Albania.

CHAPTER 1

ALBANIA:
THE LAND OF THE MERCEDES CARS

Statue of Skanderbeg, Central Square, Tirana.

The excitement started even before I left England, when the fire alarm at my airport hotel went off just as I was getting up to dress. Everyone had to rush out clad only in dressing gowns and night clothes. Luckily, it proved to be a false alarm, and we were able to return to our rooms. The flight itself was punctual, and the plane only half full. When we arrived at Tirana, we discovered there were only four of us, plus the driver of our people carrier and our Albanian guide. None of us could understand why the tour had not been cancelled for lack of take-up. My fellow passengers were a married couple and another widower, younger than me.

The hotel we were taken to, only a quarter of a mile from the central square of Tirana, was small and clean. When I entered my room, I found on the dressing table the following notice, which I have produced with the exact English grammar, punctuation, and spelling of the original.

INTERNAL REGULATION OF THE HOTEL TAFAJ

For costumer

1. The client has to show the identification card and than register
2. The client has to show and deposit, as shown by the receipt all his valuable objects at the reception, otherwise the hotel accepts no responsibilities.

About the hotel

1. The owner has to give the costumer the room booked according to the price and accommodation period until the determined date.
2. The owner has to put at the costumer's disposal the room booked from him at 18 of the date of his arrival, or except to any delay in case there has been an announcement.
3. The room is available for the costumer the 14 of the date of arrival to 12 of the departure date.
4. No matter when the client comes to the hotel the date is regarded and rescored as a full date of the accommodation. Conceding the rooms for rent on hourly basis is not allowed.
5. The client is not allowed to:
   Cook and consume in the room, without requesting room service, unless the costumer is ill, Doing laundry in the room and hanging it out of the window, throwing away litter or rigid objects out of the window, using electrical equipment, fuel or gas, making holes in the walls to hang pictures or other objects.
6. The customer has to pay the determined price in advance on special agreement. The costumer has to pay for the accommodation according to the agreement with the hotel owner in the moment of registration, one day earlier or the moment of the departure. The costumers without luggage have to pay the whole amount of money in the moment of registration. The hotel owner has to provide the costumer with bills for every service offered in payment. If the costumer has to leave before 2 am the receptionist has to announce the time. The costumer can pay cash, by credit card, or in foreign currency according to the exchange rate determined to the reception. Luggage or any other mislaid objects when identified by the hotel owner can be kept for a deadline of 60 days from the date of the customer's departure.
7. The implementation of the regulation's provisions is obligatory for both, the costumer and hotel owner. For any problems with the accommodation, room service, the receptionist and the hotel owner have to be announced. The hotel owner must accomplish the determined sanctions until the date of the costumer's departure from the hotel.

We had a small but pleasant meal that evening, although the dining room had several cages in which birds and small animals were held in very cramped conditions.

The next day, the weather was perfect: sunny and with a temperature of 23 degrees Celsius by ten o'clock. The morning was spent in exploring the central area of Tirana, in the main not an inspiring city. The traffic, especially in the central square, was appalling, and every other car seemed to be a Mercedes, frequently of rather ancient vintage. None of the inhabitants could, or would, explain where they had come from. In the centre of the square stood a statue of Skanderbeg, their great national hero. Just off the square was a remarkable painted mosque. Hoxha had tried to destroy or put to other uses all religious buildings, and yet this mosque had retained its paintings on all its internal walls. The only other similar painted mosque I had seen before was not far away in what is now the former Yugoslav Republic of Macedonia. How this mosque had escaped the hands of the tyrant, I do not know. The frescos in both of these buildings are remarkable.

Frescos in Tirana mosque.

Also in the square, there was a remarkably good bookshop, where I was able to obtain *The Laws of Lek*, which covers all the details of what was involved in the notorious blood feuds which had existed throughout the country well into the twentieth century (they are believed to still exist today in some of the remoter parts of the country). I had not realised that the blood feud was itself governed by such strict and complicated laws, which seem to have been remarkably well obeyed.

We were quickly recognised as foreigners, who were still something of a rarity in most parts of Albania, and were the objects of much interest, especially to the children, who usually wanted to practice their English and have their photographs taken. They never pestered us for money or sweets, which is too common in some Middle Eastern countries.

We were next driven to the Martyr's Cemetery, on a hill overlooking Tirana. Here there were hundreds of tombs of partisan heroes, the tombstones all being flat on the ground, unlike an English churchyard with its stones standing up. The whole area was dominated by a huge statue of the Spirit of Albania. At the bottom of this statue was a small boy, groping around completely blinded by a large hat pulled down over his eyes. There was also a column which was supposed to house the Sacred Flame, but this was not alight and had apparently not been so for several years, since it cost too much to keep it alight. Such was the economy of what is supposed to be the poorest country in Europe, despite the number of Mercedes on the streets.

Schoolchildren in Tirana.

Child at Martyr's Cemetery, Tirana.

After lunch we drove into the mountains to Kruja, much of which was made up of ugly high rise buildings. There was still, however, one old cobbled street through which we walked (no vehicle traffic was permitted) to reach the castle, which had been turned into a museum of the hero Skanderbeg.

Old street in Kruja.

Inside the entrance, a set of steps was dominated by a huge statue of this medieval leader and some of his followers. Unfortunately, the rest of the museum held little real interest.

When we returned to Tirana, we visited the tiny Mosaic Museum, with its attractive courtyard, which held a few Roman statues as well as a few in situ mosaics. Then we went to the very attractive Roman bridge over a dried-up waterway full of litter. One was not able to get a good view of this bridge, since the new bridge had been built almost touching it. It was surprising that Hoxha had not pulled down this ancient remain, for he had destroyed so much of the old in order to build the new concrete blocks, which he considered up-to-date; many old villages were demolished in the name of modernism.

Roman bridge, Tirana.

The next day was to mark the real start of our travels, for one seldom obtains a true impression of a country from its capital city. We climbed into our vivid blue people carrier and set out to visit the large seaside resort of Durres. If we had expected the traffic problems to improve as we left Tirana, we would have been mistaken. The whole of the dual carriageway was treated by the majority of drivers as though it were a Grand Prix circuit, and they were all Formula One drivers. Our own driver was, mercifully, one of the most skilful drivers I have known, though even he had the fault of believing, mistakenly, that the other drivers had the same degree of skill as himself. The frequent traffic jams where the road was undergoing improvements were in fact a relief to us. Luckily, once we left Durres, the amount of traffic was to be considerably less.

Durres itself was a modern-looking place, with a large number of concrete tower blocks, which we were to become accustomed to seeing in many of the places we visited. Although we did not have time to stop there, our guide pointed out a large mosque up on a hill, which he said was the largest mosque in Albania. It was now once again functioning as a mosque, for under Hoxha it had been turned into a Temple of Secularism. When we reached Durres, we were driven to see the only ancient remains: the very impressive city walls and the amphitheatre.

Large mosque, Durres.   *Frescos in amphitheatre, Durres.*

A plaque there read:

This amphitheatre was built in the beginning of the second century AD. It compares favourably with the most famous theatres of antiquity. The elliptical shape with the biggest axis is more than 120 metres and a height of 20 metres. The capacity of the amphitheatre is approximately 15,000 to 18,000 spectators. In the amphitheatre, slave owners amused themselves watching fights of gladiators and beasts.

This construction represents the economic power of Dyrrachion as one of the most important cities in the Adriatic region and of the knowledge of the technically Illyrian hall.

The amphitheatre was discovered in 1966.

Unfortunately, much of the site had been built over. Possibly the most interesting part of the construction was an area where the gladiators used to assemble before making an appearance. In early Christian times, this was turned into a small chapel with frescoed walls. How long these frescos will remain visible is questionable for, despite a modern protective roof, damp and green mould have made a serious appearance, and little is being done to stop the ravages. We also visited a small but attractive archaeological museum, before being taken to the top of what was said to be the tallest building in Durres, where there was a café with an impressive view over the coast. We had a cup of very ordinary Nescafe. After this, we left the coast to drive inland into the mountains to the town of Elbasan. The quantity of traffic steadily diminished as we started up into the mountains.

This part of the journey was of special interest to me, for it took in the route (though in the reverse direction) which had been taken by Flora Sandes, a clergyman's daughter who had worked as a nurse in Serbia in 1914. When her unit was disbanded after the third invasion by the Austrians, she had joined the Serbian army as a soldier, becoming probably the only British woman who served on the front line during the First World War. During the particularly harsh winter of 1915/16, when the Serbs were eventually forced to leave Serbia and retreat to the Adriatic Sea over the Albanian and Montenegrin mountains, she took part in this retreat. At that time, there was no road at all, and even now, the road was not easy.

We reached Elbasan, where we had lunch at a restaurant just inside the old town walls. Flora Sandes described Elbasan as "a horrid little town where the cobbled streets turned to mud after rain". It rained while we were having lunch, and the streets inside the walls did turn to mud.

Outside the walls, however, change had been great. Hoxha had decided that it would become the industrial centre of Albania, and many factories had been built. The resulting pollution was so great that it had received the nickname of "the Purple Town", because when it rained, the water turned purple. Since the death of Hoxha, all the factories except one had become derelict, and although our rain was not purple, the whole effect was most depressing.

After lunch, we climbed through rain, sleet, and a little snow up over a high mountain pass; I found it difficult to imagine how Flora Sandes and the army, with almost no food, no proper clothing, and no roads (in some places, there was not even a track), had managed the journey at all, though one must remember that thousands died of cold and hunger during the retreat.

Eventually, we crossed the pass and started descending towards Lake Ohrid. As we descended, the sky cleared, and we found ourselves once more in bright sunlight. We had a long wait crossing the frontier into the former Yugoslav Republic of Macedonia, for there was a lengthy delay before being allowed to leave Albania. Apparently, some of our paperwork was not to the liking of the local officials. However, we were eventually allowed to depart and descended to the lake and town of Ohrid. Here, we found that the driver had no directions to the hotel. Luckily, I had been there some three years previously and was able to show him the way, despite some new one-way streets. The hotel was only about a hundred metres from where Jacynth and I had stayed on our previous visit and had equally lovely views over the lake.

I had been facing the visit to Ohrid with some trepidation for two reasons. The first was that it had been one of the favourite towns that Jacynth and I had visited on several occasions, and I was not sure how I would react to her not being with me. The other was that our whole day there would be on foot; would I be able to keep up with my companions at my greater age? I needed have no apprehension on either account. I soon found that the memories recalled from previous visits were all happy, and though of course I missed her greatly, seeing the things we had enjoyed together merely seemed to be an extension of our time together. This was a feeling I continued to have during my later travels. As for my physical strength, I found I was every bit as fit as my companions.

Before we had supper, I walked to the front of the Millennium Hotel, where I had stayed on my previous visit, and was sad to see it had become rather shabby. I was even sadder to see that the memorial to the Dutch poet Den Doolard, situated opposite the Millennium Hotel, the official opening ceremony of which I had attended three years earlier, was also looking neglected, with uncleared litter lying around it. It was interesting that this was almost the only litter I saw during this brief visit outside Albania, where it is everywhere.

We had an excellent supper at our hotel. My room was spotlessly clean, and the loo top had a paper cover with the word "Desinfacted" printed in large letters on it.

Church of St Jovan at Kaneo, Ohrid.

We woke the next morning to a cloudless sky and a perfect temperature, which rose to just 20 degrees at its highest, lovely for walking. Our local Ohrid guide appeared, and we started by walking along the lakeside for the better part of a mile to the old town, where we boarded a small rickety boat with a rusty outboard motor to take us to the peninsular church of St Jovan at Kaneo. This church was beautiful from the outside, in the loveliest position of almost any church I've seen, with a wonderful view across the lake to the Albanian mountains. The inside, though, is not much out of the ordinary, despite some good frescos, and we were each given a glass of excellent Raki by the monk in charge. On previous visits, we had driven by car, but now road traffic was forbidden, and most visitors arrive by boat rather than do the fairly long land walk. On our return journey, our outboard motor stopped, and we drifted helplessly for a time, before the boatman managed to get it functioning and took us to the old town.

We then climbed the steep cobbled street, first to the attractive small Roman theatre, and then on to the church Mother of God Peribleptos, more commonly known as St Clement.

Church of St Clement, Ohrid.

This was one of my favourite Orthodox churches. From outside, it looked like a very attractive large church, but nothing extraordinary. However, inside, the walls were covered with some of the most marvellous frescos, dating from the thirteenth to the sixteenth centuries, that I had ever seen. I was pleased to see the curator Jacynth and I had met on our previous visit, and to my surprise, she clearly remembered that occasion. She added that she had published the book on frescos that she had been working on when we had talked with her before. Unfortunately, the stock in the shop had sold out, but she said that if I would like it, she would send her son down to our hotel that evening with a spare copy she still had at home. In due course, the young man arrived with the lovely book, for which he would only accept half the published price.

After a long look at the frescos, we crossed the churchyard to the Icon Museum. On our first visit to Ohrid, the icons had been displayed in the narthex of the church, but now this museum had been built for them. It claimed to be the finest icon museum in the world, and regardless of whether this claim is justified, it had a most marvellous collection of icons dating from the eleventh century. There were several exhibits from its collection in a recent large icon exhibition in London, and there was more than enough variety to give the lie to those many people who say that all icons look alike. Indeed, Ohrid is worth visiting for the Church of St Clement and the Icon Museum alone.

After retracing our steps downhill to the main town, we visited the Cathedral Church of St Sophia, which had been built in the eleventh century on the remains of a former basilica. Under the Ottomans, it first became a mosque and later a warehouse and finally once again a Christian church, after the expulsion of the Turks in 1912. The earlier whitewash has been removed to reveal the eleventh-century frescos. On this occasion the gallery, which is not normally open to view, was unlocked specially for us so that I was able to see, for the first time, the frescos there as well as in the main body of the church.

Cathedral Church of St Sophia, Ohrid.

After lunch, we were free to do what we wanted. I walked around the lovely Ottoman town, visited a small art gallery, and then went to a place where they were making handmade paper, where I bought a small drawing of the cathedral, drawn on a sheet of this paper. I then walked along the promontory towards St Jovan and visited St Clement's Monastery Church, a new church only completed in 2003, built beside St Clement's own monastery school, started in AD 293, and where his body was originally buried, until the building was turned into a mosque and his body was transferred to the other St Clement. The whole site was still being excavated, and a section of an old Roman road, in excellent condition, had been uncovered, as well as several mosaics, still in situ, and a large number of graves, suggesting that it was also a hospital in St Clement's time.

I had another view of St Jovan before climbing up the steep hill to the castle, which overlooked Ohrid and the lake, and where I had never been before. Little remained of this building, built by the Turks, except for the fine walls. However, the walk proved well worthwhile for the very fine view, especially with the number of Judas and fruit trees in full blossom.

Ohrid. Ohrid.   *View from citadel.*

The next day, we started by travelling down the lake to the monastery of St Naum, right on the Albanian border. I had forgotten that after a long drive by the lakeside, the road went inland and uphill before descending again to the lake about a mile from the monastery. At this point, everything had changed since my last visit. Instead of driving along to the monastery, we were first stopped at a barrier to pay an entrance fee and then made to park and walk the rest of the way to the monastery between a large number of stalls selling tourist tat. How they did in the stalls, I do not know, for there were very few tourists there or at the monastery. Fortunately, the church, with its marvellous frescos, was still the same, except that the number of peacocks seemed to have considerably increased; we had a good show of them displaying their tails as well as seeing fine views from the monastery over the lake and to the snow-covered mountains. The little chapel below the monastery hill was in scaffolding for restoration, so we were not able to see inside.

St Naum Church, Lake Ohrid.

We were given enough time to see everything before reboarding our transport and crossing the frontier, this time without any delays, back into Albania, where we stopped for a lunch of freshly caught Ohrid trout. In Ohrid town itself, the catching of these superb fish was now officially forbidden, although a blind eye was turned to a few families whose ancestors had been catching them for generations for consumption in the family restaurant, but there seemed to be no such restriction in the Albanian part of the lake. Another difference from Macedonia was the amount of litter we once again encountered.

We had been warned that the road to Korca was very bad, and it might take three hours to drive the comparatively short distance. In fact, the road had just been upgraded and was one of the few good roads we encountered, so that we took less than an hour.

The old hotel in Korca, stayed in by Byron.

The Grand Hotel where we stayed was not particularly grand, but it was perfectly acceptable and well situated on the main square. Some of the old houses in the town had been lost, but since the death of Hoxha, others have been well restored. We visited an old hotel in the market, supposedly stayed in by Byron. All I can say is that if it was in the state it now was, Byron himself must have been shocked, for the yard was a litter dump and the whole place looked filthy, yet there were still people living there.

We also saw what was possibly the oldest mosque in the whole of the Balkans and a large modern Romanian Orthodox church, with a Romanian patriotic statue in front; we were given pieces of greenery representing palm leaves, for it was the day before their Palm Sunday. There was also a remarkable museum of icons almost rivalling that in Ohrid, and an Edith Durham Street. Edith Durham was the British expert on Albania at the start of the twentieth century; she is remembered in Albania as a great hero, while almost forgotten in Britain. Our guide was most impressed that I not only knew who she was but also possessed several books written by her. So he thought that I must be a real expert on Albania, and whenever he didn't know something, he would always ask me, addressing me as "Professor", which was embarrassing to me, since one of my companions was a real professor (though luckily in an unrelated subject).

Later, we walked some distance to a restaurant for what was supposed to be a light supper. If this was "light", I dread to think how much would appear for a full meal there. Beside the excellent food, there was also very good wine.

The next morning, our Easter Day in the UK, started sunny, though by lunch time, it had clouded over, and the weather looked ominous. We started by visiting a highly mechanised beer factory, which was supposed to produce the best beer in Albania. At the end of the tour, we were each given a large glass of their product, which tasted excellent, even at that early hour.

The Albanian beer factory in Korca.

We then drove to the nearby village of Mjorba, where we found the delightful small St Mary's Church, said to be the oldest church in the Balkans. The outside was very attractive, made of local stone, but the anti-earthquake timber coursing gave no hint at the marvellous frescos inside. They were some of the best early frescos I had ever seen, right up to the best in the churches in what used to be Yugoslavia. This church had another advantage: there were no restrictions on photography.

Frescos in St Mary's Church, Mjorba.

Exterior of St Mary's Church, Mjorba.

After this, we drove over unmade-up roads to the village of Voskopoja. It was hard to imagine now that in the early eighteenth century, this was one of the largest cities in the Balkans, with some 35,000 inhabitants, compared with its present population of a few hundred peasant farmers living in its decaying houses and litter-ridden muddy streets.

Voskopoja.

St Nicholas Church, Voskopoja.

In 1720, the first permanent printing press was established there in the Balkans, and an important academy existed for training artists to produce frescos and icons. One of its twenty-four churches, St Nicholas, was still worth seeing for both the internal and external frescos. On the way there, we also visited a large but primitive cattle market selling horses, donkeys, and sheep as well as cattle. The only real colour was a car, an ancient Mercedes, decorated for a wedding.

From Voskopoja, it was a fairly short drive, past a very impoverished village, to the shores of Lake Prespa, which was also bordered by Greece and the former Yugoslav Republic of Macedonia.

Lake Prespa, with approaching storm.

Village near Lake Prespa.

Jacynth and I had visited the lake before from both of these countries. A village there in northern Greece had the most remarkable cottage architecture but was also the poorest and most primitive village I visited in that country. Overlooking the lake from Macedonia was a solitary church, which looked just like a barn from the outside but contained some marvellous frescos on the inside. Indeed, this area of the Balkans had an extraordinary number of churches decorated in this way, many of the frescos dating from well before the Renaissance. The lake had changed colour from its normal blue to grey and dark under a lowering black sky, which looked ominously like heavy rain to come.

The next day, the weather had well and truly broken. This was a great pity, for it was to be our longest journey, much of it through what would have been, in better weather, spectacular mountain and woodland scenery in very wild country. As it was, we only caught occasional glimpses through the driving rain and mist.

Tepelene village.

The quality of the road surface was unspeakably dreadful, and it was no surprise when at one point, we were held up for half an hour by a Mercedes which had collided with a local bus. The police had not yet arrived, but those already present were struggling to move the damaged vehicles to the side of the road. They eventually succeeded, so we were able to edge past and never found out how the police would have behaved when, and if, they did appear.

Luckily, the rain ceased for a time at our lunch stop in a small mountain town, where there was a huge rock towering over a mosque and a river. There was also a small war memorial decorated with brightly coloured flowers and, standing by them, an empty beer bottle.

Then we drove to visit Girocastra, an Ottoman town. We climbed up to the citadel in a damp drizzle. A military museum had been established in the fortress, and it included an American military plane which had been shot down in 1957when it strayed by mistake into Albanian air space. In good weather, the views from the citadel must have been spectacular.

Citadel of Girocastra.

View of Girocastra from citadel.

The old town itself was full of interesting buildings. One Albanian wrote in the year 2000:

> 'It was a steep city, perhaps the steepest in the world . . . . Because of its steepness it would come about that at the roof level of one house you would find the foundations of another, and certainly this was the only place in the world where if a passer-by fell, instead of sliding into a roadside ditch, he might end up on the roof of a tall house. This is something the drunkards knew better than anyone. It was a very surprising city. You could be going along a street and, if you wanted, you could stretch your arm out a bit and put your hat on top of a minaret.'

This may be an exaggeration, but it certainly was a delightful town. While we were looking round the old town, we also visited Hoxha's birthplace, which had been turned into a museum showing the inside of a typical Ottoman house.

Then on to the port of Saranda, where we were to stay for two nights. This was where Jacynth and I had come on a day trip from Corfu a few years before, when we went to see the Roman site of Butrint, which I was to see again the next day.

Roman Butrint.

Roman Butrint.

There was apparently a great thunderstorm during the night, but I had slept soundly through it. However, it was still pouring heavily the next morning when we set off for Butrint. A telephone call to the local guide there told us that it had just stopped raining, and when we arrived, this proved to be true. The skies gradually cleared, and we were to have good weather for the remainder of our Albanian trip. Butrint again proved to be an attractive site, though nothing as fine as the local literature would suggest. Above the main Roman site, which was very susceptible to flooding, some of the walls on the cliff leading up to the castle were made of huge multi-shaped stones, which fitted tightly together without any need of cement, like some of the walls found in ancient places in South America. The little theatre was sometimes used for modern-day performances. The lovely mosaic flooring in the baptistery was now hidden by gravel-covered plastic sheeting, so one had to be content with seeing it in a little booklet.

We climbed up to the citadel, where I had not been on my previous visit, and found a well-arranged museum as well as a superb view in several directions, showing how close we were to Corfu. I also found that the local guide had been taught at school by Aphrodite, the superb and kindly guide of my previous visit.

We lunched in a restaurant in another citadel overlooking Saranda, a town which had more than doubled in size since my previous visit. However, some huge new buildings were being demolished for being built without planning permission, which was now firmly, if belatedly, being demanded and enforced.

The afternoon was free, so I was able to walk through the town and visit the ruins of a large basilica and synagogue. For the one and only time on our visit, we were grossly overcharged for our wine at dinner. The owners of the restaurant said the price on the menu was a mistake and insisted that we pay the real price instead, though most of us believed it was a purposeful fraud. The price was in fact only the price one would have expected to pay at a good restaurant in the UK, but elsewhere in Albania, the cost was only a third of that.

The next day, we set off again up to the north. Much of the time in the first part of the journey, we kept to the coast, though the road (whose quality varied from the occasional excellent to the more frequent abysmal) sometimes climbed to a height of over 1,000 metres, giving lovely views. Our first stop was to see the castle built by the notorious Ali Pasha of Joanina, who had at one time been visited by Byron, who had dressed up in Albanian clothes for the visit. This was a fascinating place, for the castle was situated on a small promontory and surrounded by yellow flowering shrubs. It was still in excellent condition, for though it had not been lived in for some years, the only damage had been done by some Greek cannon balls against the Italians, who had occupied it during the Second World War. After the war, it had been used as a prison, and a number of the walls were still decorated by the prisoners' graffiti.

Further on, we stopped for lunch at a restaurant overlooking a mile-long beach of fine sand, with no one on it at all, despite it being sunny and warm; three fishermen were busy repairing their fishing nets, not far from two of the concrete pillboxes, built by Hoxha, which we found all over the country. Indeed, there were said to be one for every four inhabitants

The castle built by Ali Pasha.

Fishermen on the beach.

of Albania. We ate an excellent fish lunch with a very good wine (which cost only a quarter of that in the previous night's meal). Then on to the town of Vlora, which was where Albania was first declared an independent nation during the first Balkan War. We visited the Museum of National Independence, small but well laid out and interesting, as well as an old mosque attributed to Sinan. We also celebrated the seventy-second birthday of Tom, one of our small group, with a cake and some good wine.

After one night in the simple but spotlessly clean hotel, we left to drive inland, over very mixed-quality roads, under a cloudless sky to the Roman site of Apollonia. This was to my mind far more attractive than Butrint. The whole area was set on a hill, with part of the remains set on a second hill overlooking the temple, and with a fine view from everywhere over the plain. The whole area was carpeted with the most beautiful wild flowers. There was a complete lack of traffic; indeed, the only vehicles I saw during the whole of our visit were a cart being pulled by a horse and a decrepit white van.

Temple at Apollonia.

Life at Apollonia.

View of Apollonian temple from café.

At the very top of the hill was a small café, where we were able to sit basking in the sun and admiring the view over the plain and towards the sea.

Museum Church, Apollonia.   *Museum Church, Apollonia.*

A small church on the site had been turned into a very attractive museum, displaying some of the statues discovered there. The start of the plain below the site was filled with flocks of sheep, geese, and goats, guarded by dogs and obviously belonging to a primitive village nearby. There were also the ruins of a Nymphaeum, with water channels leading down the hillside to it. While I climbed up to see this, the rest of the party went off to look at some of the ubiquitous pill boxes and managed to get into one of them.

We travelled on and stopped for lunch at a restaurant up a steep hill above the plain. This was followed by a visit to a working monastery, with some good frescos. I was interested to see that the Dormition of Mary had the virgin dressed in red rather than the usual blue (I do not know why). Our next stop was for wine tasting at what was reputed to be the best vineyard in the country: a most enjoyable experience. Then on to Berat, another Ottoman town which is, I think, much more attractive than the better known Girocastra, though the lovely weather may have influenced my views.

Before supper, I took a walk in the evening sunshine along the river bank. There was a beautiful bridge across the river and many fine Ottoman houses on both banks.

Bridge at Berat.

We spent much of the next day exploring Berat before returning to Tirana. There was a fine Tekke and old mosque not far from the river, as well as a small church. A little up the hill was a museum in an old house, showing what it would have been like living there a hundred years before.

Mosque, Berat.

House Museum, Berat.

We were then driven up to the citadel well above, and with fine views of, the town and across to the mountains. There were also two delightful churches, one of which we could not enter, since it was being prepared for a wedding.

Citadel, Berat.

Wedding party, Berat.

There were a number of interesting buildings, including an attractive Ottoman house inside the citadel. After seeing them, we were driven back to our hotel in Tirana, from where we went and travelled in a teleferique, with rather decrepit cabins, up a mountain with good, if misty, views over the city. Some of the mountainside houses which we travelled above looked as if they had come out from the Middle Ages.

Teleferique, Tirana.

View from teleferique.

The next day was to be our last, for we were to be flying home in the evening, but it was still to be an interesting one. First, we went to visit an old Bektasi Tekke with four tombs, which were being guarded by an old lady who had protected them during the Hoxha years and was herself a descendant of one of these early Bektases. Then after going to a covered bazaar, we paid a visit to the international headquarters of the Bektases. Unfortunately, we were not able to visit the church itself, since it was being restored, but a senior priest appeared and gave an interesting talk about the sect.

Bektasi priest.

We then travelled to the ruins of a nearby mountaintop castle; some of the ruins had been turned into a restaurant, and we had lunch. The whole was reached by climbing up a rough path, interspersed with over three hundred steps, to reach it. Luckily, the food was good, and it made a fitting end to an exciting holiday.

Mountaintop restaurant.

CHAPTER 2

ISTANBUL: A CITY ON TWO CONTINENTS

Sultan Ahmet Mosque (the Blue Mosque).

My next trip later in the same year was to be of a very different nature. I took my daughter, Elinor, and her identical twins, Alexandra and Natacha, who had both just finished their first year at university, Alexandra reading veterinary science at Nottingham and Natacha history at Cambridge. I knew Istanbul quite well. Jacynth and I first went there in 1973, taking Elinor and a school friend of hers with us. That was a time when there were few hotels and few tourists, except for backpackers, and we had come to love it, and Turkey, over the years, despite the tremendous changes that had taken place. For this visit, I did not make an itinerary as such but just a list of some of the places I felt we should visit; we would decide what to do and when, according to how things panned out. I booked us in at the Hotel Avicenna, which was an old Turkish house turned into an hotel, and which was situated most conveniently a quarter of a mile from the Sultan Ahmet Mosque (the Blue Mosque) and the Hippodrome. The most famous monument in the Hippodrome itself is the Egyptian Obelisk, whose carvings look completely new despite its age of some 3,500 years. Also interesting is the stone block on which it stands, which show carvings of it being erected after it was imported to Istanbul in the fourth century AD. The Hippodrome is really the centre of the old city, since St Sophia Church, the Grand Bazaar, the Mosaic Museum, the museum quarter, and the Topkapi Palace are all situated close by, with several other sites within easy reach.

The Egyptian Obelisk.

Base of the Egyptian Obelisk.

We did not have an easy time at the airport in Istanbul. We knew we had to obtain visas on arrival but assumed we got them at the passport desk, as was the case in Northern Cyprus. Unfortunately, we arrived at the same time as several other planes, so we had to queue for a long time before reaching the desk, where we were informed we had to obtain our visas at another kiosk, which of course was situated on the opposite side of the passport desk. We then had an equally long queue to obtain our visas, before returning to the passport area. Luckily, a kindly official had seen what had happened and called us to the front of the queue.

After picking up our luggage, we took a taxi to the hotel. Istanbul taxi drivers vary greatly in skill and honesty. It is important to make sure that the meters are set at zero before starting out, for some drivers occasionally try to start off with quite a sum already entered. It is also useful to let slip that you have visited the city before, so he will not be tempted to take a longer and more expensive way round. Our driver took us by the most direct route. There are many very honest drivers; I remember one time when we were being driven to one of the lesser sites when I pointed out to the driver that he should have turned off at the last turning. He assured me that he knew the best way. Later on, he admitted he was lost, and it took him some time to find the right way. When we eventually arrived, he said that it was entirely his fault and would only accept half the meter fare, despite the fact that this was quite a bit less than it would have been if he had gone direct.

That evening, we had a very good dinner in the rooftop restaurant of the hotel, with views across to the Asian side of the Bosphorus, where we could easily see the Scutari barracks of Florence Nightingale fame. The sides of this huge building were about a quarter of a mile long; it is still in use as barracks. Recently, a father and son were billeted in the barracks at the same time, and such was the size of the place they never saw each other the whole of that time. It was possible to visit the Florence Nightingale museum in two little rooms in one of the towers, but arrangements had to be made well in advance, and as I had been there twice in the past, we did not take time out to visit this time.

The next day, after an excellent breakfast in the courtyard downstairs restaurant, we began our real holiday.

Alexandra and Natacha with St Sophia in the background.

Our first visit was to Sultan Ahmet, or the Blue Mosque, as it is usually called by the English. This was a magnificent building from the outside, with six minarets, but I was slightly disappointed inside, despite the lovely blue tiles on the pillars and walls. The proportions, to me, were not as fine as several other Turkish mosques, and the columns rather thick and clumsy for the height.

The next building, on the contrary, was even finer on the inside than it was on the outside. St Sophia was dedicated by Emperor Justinian in AD 537 and remained a church for nearly a thousand years, until Constantinople fell to the Turks in 1453. It then served as a mosque for nearly five hundred years until 1935, when it was turned into a museum by Ataturk. I have never seen, or yet managed to take, a photograph which gives any real idea of the space and openness one finds inside. The nearest to showing this are some drawings by one of the Fossati Brothers, Swiss architects who did extensive restorations in the late 1840s.

Interior of St Sophia.

This is undoubtedly one of the greatest buildings in the world. Many visitors do not walk up to the balconies and so miss an awful lot. The walk up was wide and not too steep. Indeed, it is said that an empress used to ride a horse up there, though I doubt this story, for I think the roof is rather too low for such a feat. The balconies, which go round three sides of the building, are each the size of a large church. There is a marvellous view down to the floor as well as up to the dome. The finest of the mosaics are also to be found up here. It is frequently said that the mosaics were all covered with whitewash when the building was turned into a mosque. However, Lady Wortley Montague, who managed, with difficulty, to obtain permission to visit the building in March 1717 (when her husband was ambassador to the Sublime Porte), wrote in a letter to a friend:

'I can't be informed why the Turks are more delicate on the subject of this mosque, than on any of the others where what Christian pleases may enter without scruple. I fancy they imagine, that, having been once consecrated, people, on pretence of curiosity, might profane it with prayers, particularly to those saints, who are still very visible in Mosaic work, and no other way defaced but by the decays of time; for it is absolutely false, though universally asserted, that the Turks defaced all the images that they found in the city'

Mosaic of John the Baptist and Christ.

Mosaic showing Empress Eirene with Mary and Jesus.

One of the balconies was cut in half by a remarkable marble screen carved in the form of two double doors with skilfully ornamented panels, which are now called the Gates of Heaven and Hell.

The church itself was orientated in the usual west-to-east directions. Looking down from the gallery, one can clearly see how this caused difficulty for the Turks when they turned it into a mosque, for the mihrab always has to face towards Mecca which is to the southeast of Istanbul, and so the mihrab had to be put at an angle to the main church.

The church had many alterations outside. Four minarets had been erected, one of them by the great Ottoman architect, Sinan, who also built some buttresses to protect the church from damage in the case of the frequent earthquakes which sometimes hit the city.

Only a few hundred yards from St Sophia, along a side street on the opposite side of the main road, was a small, unprepossessing building which is the entrance to one of the most unusual sites in Istanbul: the Yerebaten Saray, the most visited of the several underground cisterns of the city. The first time I visited here, one just saw a few steps with a roll of barbed wire across them leading down to the water, with a half-submerged decrepit rowing boat, beyond which it was possible to discern tall columns fading away into the gloom. The interior was now far more open. The whole was reasonably lit, and there were wooden walkways which take you around the whole 140-metre-long and 70-meter-wide cistern with its 336 columns to the far end, where the last two columns are standing on Roman heads, one of them upside down and the other sideways on. There were a large number of fish swimming in the water and music echoed around. This particular cistern dated from AD 532.

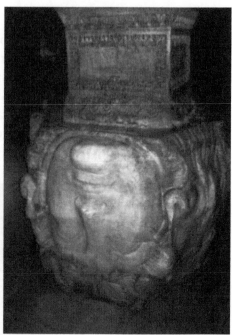

Column in Yerebaten Saray.   *Column base in Yerebaten Saray.*

On another occasion, we walked along the east side of St Sophia to visit the Topkapi Palace, which lies a little to the north. The narrow entrance gate through the wall to the first court was just beyond a very fine fountain.

Fountain of Ahmet 111.   *Church of St Eirene.*

Immediately inside the first court was the Church of St Eirene, which is older than St Sophia. On my first visit, it was a military museum, but since that had been moved away, it was usually closed except for the occasional classical concert (one of which I attended and found the acoustics very fine). Unfortunately, it was not open at all during this visit.

The rest of the very large first court was now lawn and trees until one reached the entrance of the second court, where there were several one-storey buildings acting as ticket offices and shops. Besides buying tickets for the Topkapi, we had to buy separate tickets for the Harem. Luckily, visits to the Harem are now individual, so that you no longer have to time things to take an English-speaking tour. We had come fairly early and made straight for the Harem so as to be able to see it while it was still not too full. Possibly because of the extra expense, a lot of the tours do not visit the Harem, despite the fact that it houses some of the finest rooms and courtyards in the whole palace.

The Harem, Topkapi.

The Harem, Topkapi.

When we had satisfied ourselves that we had seen enough in the Harem, we went round the rest of the palace which was, as we expected, very crowded. Unfortunately, we were not able to see the kitchens with their marvellous collection of ceramics, since they were closed for restoration, but we were able to see most other areas with their valuable exhibits.

Family in the Topkapi.

The Topkapi.

Some way down the steep hill from the Topkapi, towards the Golden Horn, was a level area with three museums which we visited. The largest of these was the Archaeological Museum, with a very fine collection of ancient remains. On the opposite side of the courtyard was the delightful little Cinili Kiosk (or Tile Museum), believed to be the oldest surviving Ottoman building in Istanbul, with its fine collection of Turkish tiles as well as some attractive stained glass windows. On the same side as the Cinili Kiosk, but nearer to the entrance of the compound, was the Museum of the Ancient Orient, with some Hittite remains as well as pre-Islamic items from different parts of the Ottoman Empire.

In the Archaeological Museum.

The Cinili Kiosk.

Elinor sitting by the Sokollu Mehmet Pasa Mosque.

From the other end of the Hippodrome, we walked down a steep street to see the Sokollu Mehmet Pasa Mosque, one of the smallest and most beautiful mosques built by the great Ottoman architect, Sinan. Here I startled the person in charge by asking if I might turn the two columns by the mihrab. These are designed to turn in normal circumstances, but if there has been an earthquake and the foundations have been damaged, they will not turn. I was allowed to turn them and show that the building was safe. I was also able to point out the small bit of black stone from the sacred Kaaba at Mecca, which was embedded above the entrance door. The light blue tiles in the mosque, the other painted decorations, the lovely soft stone, and the sense of space and balance made this one of my favourite buildings in the city.

A further walk downhill brought us to the courtyard of the church of Sts. Sergius and Bacchus (often called Kucuk St Sophia). This church was built some twelve years before St Sophia was started and is now a mosque. The first time I visited, the courtyard housed a flock of sheep, but it was tidied up into a small café, and most of the low buildings round it were little shops. It was a small church, with a dome, and was said to have been an architectural experiment before the building of St Sophia itself. It had to undergo a number of repairs recently when cracks appeared, possibly due to vibrations caused by the railway, which runs only a few yards away. With its pale cream colour and mainly black pillars, it has lovely feel about it, and for the first time, I was allowed to climb the steep steps and see the view from the balcony.

Church of Sts. Sergius and Bacchus (Kucuk St Sophia).

We did not, however, restrict ourselves to visiting places within walking distance from the hotel. One day, we took the tram from near the Hippodrome to the west up past the rather dull burnt column to the large square just beyond the Beyazit Mosque. We then took the road which ran alongside the great covered bazaar, which we were to visit later. Our aim was to see the great Suleymaniye Mosque, possibly Sinan's greatest mosque in Istanbul (though not as fine as his masterpiece in Edirne, which dominates and can be seen from almost any part of the city). We then turned left and carried on up a steep narrow street, until we reached the mosque. Here we were in for a disappointment, since the mosque was closed for restoration, so we were only able to see the exterior and the little mausoleum that Sinan had built for himself.

View of Suleymaniye Mosque from Topkapi.

Sinan mausoleum.

We then took a taxi to another of the major sites of the city. Like St Sophia, the Church of St Saviour in Chora, or the Kariye Mosque, as it was now called, had been turned into a mosque and then into a museum. It held what were probably the finest mosaics and frescos in the city, all dating from the early fourteenth century. The fresco of the Anastasis (the Harrowing of Hell) in the Pareeclesion must be one of the greatest paintings in the world, and it was worth going to Constantinople just to see this painting alone. Because it was so far out from the centre, only a few of the tours visit it, and though it was crowded at times, it was usually possible to find a quiet period to admire what is on show.

The Anastasis in the Church of St Saviour in Chora (Kariye Mosque).

Fresco in St Saviour in Chora.

St Saviour in Chora (Kariye Mosque).

We spent a long time here, and when we eventually left, we walked beside the city wall, downhill to the Golden Horn. This part of the city was hardly visited by tourists; we found not much had changed since my first visit, except for the ruins of the Byzantine Blachernae

Palace, which had been tidied up and transformed into a garden and a small café. When we reached the bottom and crossed the busy main road to the bank of the Golden Horn, we discovered that all the little factories which used to line the bank (polluting the water and turning it a dirty purple colour) had been swept away and replaced by lawn and flower beds; the water had returned to something like it had been when it had the nickname of "Sweet Waters of Europe".

We now walked along to the suburb of Eyup. This was one of the most holy places of Islam and was crowded, not with tourists, but with pilgrims visiting the tomb of the Prophet Mahomet's friend and standard bearer. We had planned to take the steep and rough track up through a Turkish graveyard to the top of the hill and Pierre Loti's tea-house, from where there is a superb view back down the Golden Horn to the city itself. To our surprise, we found there was now a cable car, which took us up painlessly.

View of the Golden Horn.

We had intended to find somewhere to eat at Eyup, possibly at the tea-house, but to our surprise, everywhere was closed and we could not even buy a drink, because it was Ramadan; nothing would be open until sunset. Central Istanbul was a very different matter from this holy place, and all the restaurateurs and café owners there put profit above religion, especially since it mainly involved selling food to foreigners. Nowhere outside Eyup did we find any difficulty in eating at any time of day.

During our visit, we normally ate at one of the many restaurants, usually open air, which could be found in the streets around the Hippodrome, and where the food was usually of a very high standard. We had an amusing incident once when eating. I was sitting beside Natacha and opposite Alexandra and Elinor when I saw several girls walking towards us.

One of them suddenly spotted us and came rushing up, calling out to Natacha, "Fancy seeing you here." Natacha looked at her blankly, never having seen her before in her life. The girl looked very taken aback and then suddenly saw Alexandra, who had been sitting with her back to her. All was explained, for she was at Nottingham University with Alexandra and but did not know she had a sister, let alone an identical twin.

I think it was at this same restaurant that the two girls, who were reading the menu, suddenly burst out laughing when they discovered among the desserts the name "Turkish Viagra". I was later to see several spice stalls in the Egyptian Bazaar, or Spice Market, as it is often called, which also sold this same substance.

The Egyptian Bazaar.

Our return from Eyup was by taxi. Unlike the morning driver, he appeared to be training for the Grand Prix, and we were very glad when we reached the Galata Bridge in safety and were able to leave him and catch the tram up to the Hippodrome.

On another occasion, we walked across the Golden Horn on the Galata Bridge and took the Tünel, the ancient funicular, which claims to be the oldest underground railway in the world, up to the Galata Tower. The Istikal Caddesi, which runs from the tower to Taksim Square, is, in effect, the Oxford Street of Istanbul, with many modern stores. The whole area used to be the European quarter, where all the embassies were (and, indeed, many still are). There was an antique tram which ran the length of the street, which was otherwise pedestrianised (except for occasional official vehicles). We walked the whole way along, discovering on the way a Dutch church which held services in English on Sundays, so when that day came, we went back for the service and for the lunch which it gave visitors afterwards, and where Elinor and the girls saw, by chance, a couple they had met back in

England. From Taksim, we took a bus down to a small suburb on the Bosphorus which had a little market and a café, where we could sit looking at the nearby First Bosphorus Bridge and some of the water traffic.

Ortakoy Mosque and Bosphorus Bridge.

Cruise ship in Bosphorus.

We took a day trip up the Bosphorus and travelled by ferry, rather than take a tour, which visited several places on both the European and Asian sides past the Ciragan Palace, which had been a burnt-out ruin when I first saw it but was now the most expensive and luxurious hotel in the city, and the fine castle of Rumeli Hisar. The final stop was at Anadolu, near the entrance of the Black Sea, where we disembarked for a stop of three hours. We first had an excellent meal at a fish restaurant on the water front and then decided to walk up to a castle high above the town so as to get the view. Of course, despite it being in the heat of a hot day, we reached the very top and then had to rush down in order to catch the ferry back. For the first time on the holiday I felt my age, for my legs almost gave way under me at the bottom, but with the aid of another couple who helped support me, we made the ferry in time; after sitting down for a few minutes, my legs completely recovered, and I was able to walk normally again. It did, however, teach me that I must not rush too fast in the heat of the day.

Another place we visited was the Rustem Pasa Mosque, dating from 1550, and another of the works of Sinan, sitting on a platform above some shops in the maze of streets below the Grand Bazaar. It also had some very fine tiles, both inside the mosque and on its exterior walls.

We, of course, had to visit the Grand Bazaar, where the girls proved to be good at haggling. In fact, so popular was the visit that they insisted on returning another day, without me, since I decided instead to take a tram down to the Galata Bridge in order to see the Yeni Mosque, which I had not visited for some years. I much preferred its airy space to Sultan Ahmet.

We also went to see the Whirling Dervishes in an old building down near the main railway station. This was very well done but, being put on as a show for the tourists, did not have the same atmosphere as when I had seen it performed as a really religious service, with few spectators, in an old Tekke in the Pera district, which was no longer open to the public.

The Yeni Mosque.

A Whirling Dervish.

There were two other places of real interest that we visited. The first of these was on the west side of the Hippodrome and opposite Sultan Ahmet: the Palace of Ibrahim Pasa, which had been turned into a museum of Turkish and Islamic art, the Turkish equivalent of our Victoria and Albert Museum, but on a smaller scale. The other place we visited was the Mosaic Museum, which was situated behind Sultan Ahmet near a little pedestrianised bazaar street of one-storey shops. The mosaics, many of them from late Roman times, were in some cases still in situ where they were found in the ruins of the great Byzantine Palace; they were well displayed.

Mosaic in Mosaic Museum.

Manuscript in museum.

This was a busy and fascinating trip, and the girls still say, several years later, that it was their best holiday ever, and they have travelled quite a lot.

CHAPTER 3

JORDAN: A COUNTRY OF CONTRASTS

The Treasury, Petra.

My last trip in 2009 was to Jordan. This was a country that Jacynth and I had never visited, and when I saw an archaeological tour run by Saga, I decided to take it. For Saga, one has to book direct, so I phoned them up and was told there was still room. All went well until I gave my date of birth; there was a long pause before I heard the words: "Oh, are you all right on your feet, for this is quite an energetic tour?" This rather startled me since Saga was supposed to be for the more elderly generation. However, I eventually persuaded them that I was fit enough and so it proved, even though I was eight years older than anyone else on the trip.

When we reached Amman, I found we were a group about fourteen strong. Amman itself proved to be a very modern city in the main, though there were a few ancient remains, and on the first day, we were taken to see them. The Acropolis on a hill had a few columns, an archaeological museum, and the substantial remains of an Umayyad palace (including a domed building), as well as an excellent view of the city and, across a deep valley, the ancient Roman theatre.

View of Amman.

The Acropolis, Amman.

We were accompanied on the trip by a Jordanian guide (who was to remain with us for the whole of our visit), our English tour manager, and an armed policeman, who also travelled with us on all our trips except one. Since he spoke no English, we never managed to discover whether he was there to protect us or to protect the local populace from us, should we turn violent. It must have been rather boring for him, since the only people he could converse with were the guide and the excellent driver, who also remained with us for the whole of the tour. The guide was first rate; he not only spoke perfect English, he also knew a lot about all the places we visited as well as improving the long coach journeys by giving us good information about the modern Jordan.

The museum, though not large, proved to be excellent, well laid out with many ancient artefacts. To my surprise, there were also on show two pages from the Dead Sea Scrolls; I had imagined that all of these ancient manuscripts were carefully guarded in Israel.

After we had viewed the places of interest on the Acropolis, we were driven to the theatre. Though it was not a great distance, it took a surprisingly long time because of the amount of traffic on the narrow main road through the bottom of the valley. The Roman theatre itself was magnificent, the tallest and steepest classical theatre I had visited (except for the one at Pergamum in Turkey). Most of our party climbed only a few of the steps, but I was determined to get to the top and see the view. I was at the very top when I was spotted by one of the ladies in the party, who called the tour manager and said, "Look, the old man is at the top. You ought to go up and make sure he can get down again." So the poor manager, who was rather portly, had to climb up (sweating profusely, for it was rather hot), to make sure that I was not in any difficulty. In fact, I got down every bit as easily as he did, and after this event, it was decided that I knew what I was doing, and I was allowed to do it without interference.

Outside the Roman Theatre.

The Roman Theatre, Amman.

At the bottom of the theatre, on either side of the stage, were two small museums: the Folklore Museum and the Museum of Popular Traditions. In one of these, there was a stuffed camel, and since no attendant was present, two small children had taken the chance to scramble up onto its back.

The next day, we were taken out to the Roman city of Jerash.

Hadrian's Arch, Jerash.

The South Gate, Jerash.

This proved to be one of the finest Roman remains I have ever visited; it was remarkably empty, for there was only one other tour, which was not there for very long, as well as a few individual visitors. We passed Hadrian's Arch and then walked along the length of the Hippodrome to the South Gate, where we entered the city itself. The first part we arrived at was the huge oval Roman Plaza, or Forum. Though I had seen several photographs of this, I was completely unprepared for the sheer size and impressiveness of the place; the few people in there were completely lost in the space and unnoticeable (in any case, it was soon empty).

The Roman Plaza, Jerash.

To the left of the Plaza were the ruins of the Temple of Zeus, and beyond that the South Theatre, the largest and best preserved of the three theatres in the city. Here we were lucky, for we were treated to a performance by a number of local musicians playing, very skilfully, on a version of bagpipes and drums.

From the far side of the Plaza, we entered the Cardo (the main street) of the city, which runs dead straight for some eight hundred metres towards the North Gate.

The Cardo, Jerash.   *Band in Jerash Theatre.*   *Baths off the Cardo.*

On the left-hand side, as we walked along, were the well-preserved remains of shops, temples, fountains, and churches. Especially imposing, as we reached towards the end, was a monumental staircase, at the head of which stood a temple, later converted by the Christian Gerasenes into a large church. We walked on past this until we reached the North Theatre. I was one of the very few of our group who walked up to the top of this theatre, out through the back, and further up the hill to see the group of churches there and then back through the remains of the huge Temple of Artemis and down the monumental staircase to the Cardo.

Monumental stairway, Jerash.   *Lunch break, Jerash.*

After leaving Jerash, we had lunch in a little restaurant near the small bazaar just outside the entrance, before heading out to the Castle of Ajloun, with very fine views over the surrounding countryside. The castle itself had suffered much damage over the years, in particular from earthquakes, so apart from the striking outer walls and the view, there was not much else worth seeing.

On both our outward and return journeys, we passed through a fair-sized town made up of modern, cheap-looking houses. This was apparently built for refugees from Palestine who now, we were told, make up over 40 percent of the population of Jordan. We were also told that most of them still have dreams of returning to their homeland.

The next day, we were taken out to see what are called either the Desert Castles or the Desert Palaces, neither of which description is entirely true. The first of the buildings we visited was the Qasr Hraneh (Qasr Kharana). This, standing alone on a small hill and visible for miles around, looked like a picture book castle but was nothing of the sort. The round towers were solid, not hollow inside, and it would be impossible, without six-foot-long arms, to fire an arrow from the arrow slit windows. In fact, they seemed to have been designed just to give some light and air to the structure. It was now believed that the Umayyads used it as a place where they could meet the leaders of the local Bedouin tribes; it was possible that the Bedouins themselves would meet there to discuss disputes and problems.

Our next visit was to Qasr Amra, a most extraordinary building for Muslims to have built, for the frescos have such subjects as naked women, dancing girls, musicians, and hunters. This was believed to have been built by the Umayyad Caliph, Walid I, as hunting baths only a few years before the Islamic edict ordering the destruction of images was issued. Somehow, possibly because of its remoteness in the desert, these frescos were never destroyed, and after some restoration, they were remarkably well preserved. The position for this building was probably chosen for the underground spring, and there was now a modern reconstruction of the way in which water was lifted from the well.

Qasr Hraneh, Desert Castle.

Fresco in Qasr Amra.

The ticket office was situated quite a little walk from the baths and displayed a considerable amount of information about the frescos. There was also a long tent by the office, which acted as a café.

Our third and final visit was to an actual castle, Qasr Al Azraq, which was built in its present form on a much older site, in 1237. It was also used by T. E. Lawrence (Lawrence of

Arabia) during the First World War as his headquarters. Lawrence's own simple room was situated above the narrow entry door, made of two heavy stone slabs. Through the entrance was a very large courtyard containing many other rooms, stables, a mosque, a well, and in one of the towers, a door made of a huge block of basalt, which must have been opened to admit the camels used in Lawrence's campaign. The stone used to build the castle was mainly black basalt, unlike the yellow sandstone used in the other desert buildings we saw.

Qasr Al Azraq Castle.

Castle entrance.

Up till this stage, the weather had been excellent, but during the course of our return to Amman, the sky had steadily darkened, and by the time we reached our hotel, the rain had started, and it poured during the night. The next day, we were due to leave for Petra, but when we boarded the coach, we were told that we would have to alter our route, since the road had been rendered impassable by the overnight rain (on our return, we would visit the places missed on this journey). Our policeman, who had been absent from our trip to the Desert Castles, rejoined us as we set out for our first stop, one of the holy places of both Christianity and Judaism, Mount Nebo, from where Moses was supposed to have seen the Promised Land before he died. The rain had ceased, but it was still damp and misty, so we could only get an impression of what must have been a magnificent view. The Moses Memorial Church and several marquees contained a large number of Byzantine mosaics, some of them still in situ. There were also several monuments remembering a recent papal visit and a small tree with rags tied to the branches as prayers from various pilgrims, a custom that is common in the Middle East.

Mount Nebo.   *Mount Nebo.*

We then drove to a village where there was a mosaic shop. This structure covered a large space where a number of workers were busy making the mosaics, which were then put on sale. The size of the mosaics went from small wine coasters up to large table tops and wall pictures. What was remarkable about this place was that the workers were all mentally or physically handicapped. We were told that this was the only establishment in the country which employed such people. The mosaics they made were sometimes of modern designs and sometimes very skilful copies of famous old mosaics.

Mosaic Shop.

We then moved on to Madaba, which is known for its mosaics. The most famous of these, the Map of Palestine, dating from the second half of the sixth century, was still in situ on the floor of a church, but some of the other mosaics in what is called the Archaeological Park merit almost equal attention and date from Roman times to modern, for there is a mosaic school in the town which produces some surprisingly good work.

Map of Palestine mosaic, Madaba.

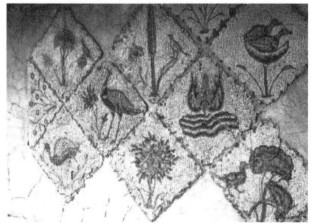

Mosaic Museum, Madaba.

We had lunch in this remarkable mosaic town. We gathered that as many as a thousand people a day visited the church to see the map mosaic but that few of them see the other sites in the town, in which case they miss out on a feast. Even our trip, and we had several hours there, seemed all too short. However, as our guide said, we had to get on to reach Petra. We did have one further stop on the way to see the outside of a very fine Crusader castle, a real castle this time, but it was closed for restoration. Our hotel near Petra had a fine view, and there was a lovely sunrise the next morning.

Shawback Castle near Petra.

Sunset over Petra mountains.

Petra proved to be an even more spectacular and larger site than I had expected. The walk from the ticket office to the entrance of the Siq itself was about half a mile. It was possible to hire a horse to ride for this distance, which none of us did, though we saw a riderless horse galloping back at one point, having evidently shed its load. It was also possible to hire a horse and carriage, seating two, to take you right through the Siq on a return journey, and several of our party opted to do this. I did not do this, for I wanted to see all that can be seen in the Siq, but I did arrange a time for meeting a carriage for the return journey. Even the walk to the entrance of the Siq itself is full of interest, with such buildings as the Obelisk Tomb to be seen. The Siq is about three-quarters of a mile long, a narrow gorge, in some places as little as six and a half feet wide, with the cliffs towering well over three hundred feet up above. In Nabatean times, it was paved, but only small sections of the paving remain, and most of the route is on smooth stabilised sand. Water channels run along the edge, and at the start, there is a small dam to prevent flooding, which was built after a flash flood in 1963 killed twenty-three tourists. There were many tombs in the multi-coloured rocks, and near the end there was a striking view of the façade of the Treasury.

Obelisk Tomb, Petra.

View of Petra Treasury from Siq.

It is only when one emerges from the Siq to the area in front of the Treasury that it is possible to gain any impression of the real site. I first went to the Treasury and looked back to the narrow gap of the Siq. It was then over a mile farther to reach the end of the main site, slightly downhill the whole way, but with cliffs and hills on one side, while on the other the cliffs, filled with tombs (some of them the height of tall temples and carved out of multi-coloured stone), make a turn away after a time. Not until one reaches the end of this main street does one start the long climb to the Monastery, as it is called. It is possible to obtain a donkey here to climb up, but I gathered the path was so steep in some parts that it was not uncommon for the rider to fall forward over the animal's head on return. None of our party took a donkey, and only four decided to climb up. I was not one of them, since I had already at one point climbed over three hundred steep steps to reach some marvellous tombs built into the cliffs, and to take in the wonderful view over the theatre and down to the great temple.

The Siq as seen from the Treasury.

A Petra tomb.

A Petra tomb.

The Theatre at Petra.

We had lunch in a café near the museum in the lower town, and then when the intrepid four started on their climb, I did a smaller diversion and climbed to visit the ruins of the Petra Church. This building has in its two side aisles some remarkable floor mosaics of the Byzantine era, showing a range of animals, birds, and people, one of which (which is rather surprising for a church) showed a bare-breasted woman. I then walked back up the main street, calling in on a shop on the way to collect a small glass phial, in which they had made a geometrical pattern of different coloured sands, the colours being taken from the colours of the Petra rocks.

Mosaic in the Petra Church.   *A Petra view.*

The next day, we began our return towards the Dead Sea, where we were to spend two nights. I personally would have liked to spend another day in Petra to get up to the Monastery, and there was plenty on the lower level I would have liked to explore more fully. The road we took was narrow, winding, and very steep in places, through hilly and attractive country, and I could fully understand why the coach had not been allowed to travel this route after heavy rain. We made one stop at a place called Kerak to see the first Crusader castle to have been built in Trans Jordan. This was perched on a steep hill and was much restored, but it must have been easy to defend both from its dramatic position and from its very strong defensive walls.

A small military museum had been formed inside one of its rooms. When I was looking at some exhibit, I overheard two of our ladies, hidden from me by a partition, talking: "You remember that place in Greece where the women threw themselves and their babies over a cliff to avoid being captured by the Turks? Well, we were told the name of the Turkish sultan at that time, but I cannot remember who it was."

"Nor can I," replied her companion. "We must ask Dermot. He will probably know."

I was surprised at the reputation I had evidently gained but did my best when asked the question a few minutes later. After dismissing several sultans who I was pretty sure were not ruling at that time, I said I thought it might possibly be Suleyman the Magnificent and was greeted with "That's it. That's the name we were told. What an incredible memory you have." I did not like to say that it was pure luck and not memory that I had given the correct answer, but I was clearly considered a fountain of knowledge by the two ladies involved.

We later drove down to the road running along the side of the Dead Sea and stopped at one point to be shown a pillar of rock above the road, which was supposed to be the famous pillar of salt into which Lot's wife had been turned when she stopped and looked back at the burning cities of Sodom and Gomorrah. We reached our hotel at the head of the lake during the afternoon and were in plenty of time to see the sunset.

Landscape near Dead Sea. *Lot's Wife Pillar.* *Kerak Castle.*

The whole of the next day was spent at this hotel. To walk along the busy road outside was not at all pleasant. I spent some time floating on my back in the Dead Sea doing a *Times* Su Doku puzzle before going and desalting myself in the hotel pool. While it was a good hotel with large grounds and gardens, I did feel it would have been much better to have spent only one night there and one more in Petra.

The Dead Sea. *Sunset over the Dead Sea.*

The next day, our final full day, we returned to Amman but visited the supposed site of the baptism of Jesus in the river Jordan on the way. The Jordan itself was now no more than a little stream in places due to the amount of water being extracted from it by other countries higher up. Indeed, the level of the Dead Sea itself was decreasing much too fast for comfort, and there was a real fear that unless something was soon done to help the Jordan, the Dead

Sea could at some stage dry up. The supposed baptismal site had changed once or twice during recent years, but there was an attractive, fairly new church, which was not by the river itself but acted as a suitable place of worship. Since this was a point where the Jordan acted as a frontier with Israel, there were several armed soldiers on both banks to make sure that none of the pilgrims, some of whom like to go into the sacred water themselves, tried to cross to the other country, for the water was shallow enough to wade across.

Church near baptismal site.

Fresco in church.

When we returned to Amman itself, we visited the Royal Automobile Museum, which housed over seventy cars and motorbikes from the personal collection of King Hussein; one car was similar to the 1928 Alvis that my father had owned after the war. All in all, an unexpected end to a very enjoyable and interesting holiday.

Fresco in Qasr.

Fresco for baptism.

Jerash theatre and band.

CHAPTER 4

UZBEKISTAN AND THE GOLDEN ROAD TO SAMARKAND

Mausoleum of Timur (Tamerlane), Samarkand.

As a chiropodist, my daughter Elinor visits patients in their own homes. One day in the spring of 2010, she found herself being quizzed by one of her patients, who had discovered she had an elderly father. The conversation went something like this:

"Your old father, does he live in an old people's home or a nursing home?"

"Oh no," said Elinor, "he still lives by himself in his own house."

"Does he have a carer who comes in regularly to make sure he is alright?"

"No. He just has a lady who comes in for two hours a week to do some cleaning for him."

"Exactly how old is he then?"

"He will be eighty-one in a few weeks time," replied Elinor.

"I imagine you will be having a big birthday party for him?"

"No."

"Why not?"

"Because he will be in Uzbekistan at that time."

Jacynth and I had visited Uzbekistan in 1997, and I had always wanted to return to see the wonderful architecture again and to visit a few other places that we had not seen on that occasion. After a comfortable night flight to Tashkent, I decided, since our group was not meeting until the afternoon, to walk out and see the fine statue of Timur (Tamerlane), which had been hidden within a small copse near the hotel of my previous visit.

Statue of Timur, Tashkent.

It was quite a long walk, and when I eventually found the statue, the copse no longer existed; it had been replaced by a rose garden, so that the statue could be viewed from a considerable distance in most directions. One of our small party said she had read on the Internet that there had been a great fuss among the locals when this change had taken place. It was considerably less romantic than it had been, but I could see the reason for the change.

In the afternoon, we were taken to see a typical covered bazaar in the city, though not the one I had visited before, when my purchases had been handed over in a plastic bag with the name and address of a butchers in Sauchiehall Street, Glasgow, printed on the outside.

That evening, we went for supper in a restaurant which was inside, of all things, a large yurt. The owner had apparently once been a nomad, so when he started up this place, he had reverted to his origins. During the course of the meal, our Uzbek guide, who was also the tour manager, made an announcement about me. He said that they were thrilled that this was my second visit to Tashkent; he also mentioned that it was my birthday. He then gave me a gift of a small ceramic figurine of an Uzbek male in country dress, which was so hideous it was rather endearing, and which I now use as a toothpick holder; the rest of the group gave a rousing rendition of "Happy Birthday to You". Needless to say, I was by some years the oldest of the group.

Part of earthquake memorial in Tashkent.

Old mosque, Tashkent.

The next day, we were taken to see the sights of the city, much of which was rebuilt (with Russian "volunteer" labour) after the centre was destroyed by a violent earthquake in April 1966. We did visit one old mosque, the surrounds of which were pulled down to rebuild a not unpleasant complex, but most of the modern Soviet architecture was hideous, despite many welcome green parks. I was amused to see outside the opera house, which was near our hotel, a poster the famous Holbein of Sir Thomas Moore from the Frick Museum (we have a very fine copy of this in Montacute).

The next day, a Sunday, we set off for Samarkand, but we had only just left the hotel car park when we were stopped by the police to see the driver's papers. Unfortunately, they found that he did not have a medical certificate to say he was fit to drive us on this tour. Apparently, they have to have a new inspection before each tour they take, and he had not had time to have a new one since his last. We had to leave the coach and walk around a nearby park for about an hour and a half until he was able to return with his new certificate.

The road to Samarkand was mainly dull and through flat land, and though the roads had improved since my previous visit, the journey was longer, for instead of cutting straight through a part of Kazakhstan, as we had done before, that road was now closed and we had to drive quite a considerable distance round that country's bulge. When we reached Samarkand itself, I was horrified at the amount of new building which had been done. Our hotel, however, was in a good position, very near the hotel I had stayed in for my previous visit, and within very easy walking distance of the Mausoleum of Timur. It was also possible to walk to the most famous square in the world, the Registan, and I was also able to walk to the fine Russian church, which is still very active and well kept.

Entrance to Timur's Mausoleum, Samarkand. *Inside Timur's Mausoleum.*

The first evening, after supper, I walked to the mausoleum and was fortunate enough to see and photograph it under floodlight. The next day, we paid our first official visit to the Mausoleum. It was a wonderful building, though very heavily restored. At the same time, it was a bit of a sham. Inside, the walls glittered in golden mosaic over the supposed tombs of Timur and some of his family. These were actually only copies of the real tombs, for he arranged to be buried in a very simple way, and it was only later that the mausoleum was built above and the replica tombs placed on the floor exactly above the real tombs. On my last visit, a curator took Jacynth and me round outside, unlocked a little door, and led us down into a very small crypt to where the real tomb was. When I told this to our guide, he said we were incredibly lucky for no one, not even the local dignitaries, were allowed down there, and it was only opened to a few very important people once every few years; he himself had never managed to gain entry there.

We boarded the coach to visit the Registan Square. To reach this, one walked down a series of steps on the open side of the square, the other three sides being surrounded by marvellous, tile-decorated buildings. Each of the large doorways led you out into other squares, themselves tile decorated, and the lower rooms of which were now shops selling musical instruments, antiques, and art. Behind the building at the far end of the square, a large blue dome of a mosque shone in the sun. When one entered this mosque, one found the walls and the inside of the dome itself were tiled with mainly blue tiles, giving a most magical effect. The whole was much restored by the Russians, and it was so well done that it was very difficult to distinguish between the old and the restored.

The Registan Square, Samarkand.

Buildings inside the Registan.

Inside of a dome in the Registan.

After we spent a long time exploring the nearly empty Registan, the coach took us on to the Shah-I-Zinda complex. There was now quite a large car park outside the walls; it used to be a narrow road. We climbed the steps to the entrance and could see the further steep steps and path between the highly decorated buildings. I myself preferred this to the Registan, for nearly all the tiles were original, even though the cemetery behind the buildings had been tidied up from its old decrepit state. I was sorry that a scribe no longer functioned from a table just inside the gate, but the atmosphere of the place was still there, even though there were more visitors than at the Registan.

Shah-I-Zinda, Samarkand.   *Shah-I-Zinda, Samarkand.*

After leaving, we walked up the hill with a fine view of the Travellers' Mosque on our right-hand side. I had never before seen this attractive-looking building, for it had previously been hidden by roadside trees, which had disappeared. Unfortunately, we did not have time to visit this mosque, for we were heading to see the Bibi-Khanym Mosque, one of the Islamic world's biggest mosques (the main gate by itself is some thirty-five metres high). I had not seen it properly before, because on my previous visit, it had been covered in scaffolding and under much-needed repair.

Travellers' Mosque, Samarkand.   *Bibi-Khanym Mosque, Samarkand.*

After supper that evening, I walked to the Registan to see it under floodlight. Most of the streets were empty, but I always felt completely safe while in Uzbekistan. The square was lovely in the lighting, but unfortunately something had happened in my camera, and I did not get any photos to come out (the next day, one of our party showed me what button to press to get it working properly again).

Our next day's visit was to Shakhrisabz, near which Timur was born and where he grew up. Much of the road to the town was being worked on, and the rest of the road was not good, to say the least, and it took us some three hours to reach the town. The main ruins of the Ak-Saray Palace were disappointing, being only a tall crumbling relic, though we did see a wedding party near it; I went up on a big wheel to obtain a view over the whole place. The most interesting place we saw was the Kok-Gumbaz Mosque, dating from 1437, behind which was the original burial complex of Timur's forebears, and even this was nothing like as fine as many of the mosques we had seen. Here, there were a few stalls in the courtyard, and I bought a rather attractive Uzbek doll for my young niece, Isabella.

On the return journey, we stopped for a time to see some villagers weaving rugs and were able to have a glimpse of country life off the beaten track.

Villager near Shakhrisabz.

Village with animal dung fuel near Shakhrisabz.

The next day, we set off on the road to Bukhara. We missed several things in Samarkand that I would have liked to see, and despite our village stop, I would have preferred to have spent the previous day back in that city. On our journey to Bukhara, we made a couple of stops, the first of which was in an attractive village where our guide wanted us to visit a famous shaman. A shaman was a person believed to have access to the world of good and evil spirits and, as a result, was supposed to have special healing powers. We spent some time walking round the village looking for her house, since she had recently moved; indeed, part of her new residence was still being built with mud-baked bricks. We all sat down, and a few of the group went over to her, individually, for some sort of blessing and a laying on of hands. I was not one of those, for time did not permit all of us being done, since we had to be moving on. Those who had the treatment said it was a weird sensation, and one person who had not been too well certainly seemed a lot better for a few days.

Building a house with mud bricks.

The shaman.

Our other break was when we were nearing Bukhara; we stopped for lunch in a small town, famous locally for its pottery, which we were able to see being made on primitive wheels and with the aid of a donkey to get rid of the bubbles in the clay.

Our hotel in Bukhara proved to be in a marvellous position; it is just visible in the back of the picture, behind the Maghoki Attar Mosque, Central Asia's oldest surviving mosque, which was built on the top of a fifth-century Zoroastrian temple (it is now used as a carpet museum).

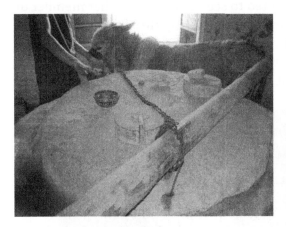

Potter's wheel turned by donkey.

Maghoki Attar Mosque, Bukhara.

Bukhara itself was a very different sort of city from Samarkand. While the main monuments in Samarkand were covered, inside and out, with the most marvellous tiles, Bukhara (which also had some wonderful tiles and blue domes) was particularly noted for its decorated, baked terra-cotta brickwork. On my previous visit, I decided that I personally preferred Bukhara, and this trip strengthened that feeling. There was also the fact that Bukhara was not modernised in the same way as Samarkand, and there were fewer ugly modern buildings. There was also a large number of craftsmen at work on stalls in the streets, producing decorated metal work, ceramics, and pictures.

Not far from the hotel was the Lyabi-Hauz Square, built round a pool where the numerous small cafés are still sheltered by ancient mulberry trees; a number of elderly Uzbek men can still be seen sitting among the tourists, playing chess. At the east end was a statue of the Hoja, the holy fool, who appears in many Sufi stories around the world, and behind that was the very fine Nadir Divanbegi Medressa.

Lyabi-Hauz Square, Bukhara.   *Nadir Divanbegi Medressa*   *Statue of Hoja.*

Another advantage of Bukhara was that much of the old city can be seen on foot and indeed was reachable from our hotel. This proved to be an excellent thing, since our guide decided to do most of our visiting in the morning to avoid the worst of the heat of the day, as temperatures in the afternoon were reaching the high thirties, which was not usual here till later in the year. This meant that I, who did not mind the heat, was able to walk out in the afternoon and see the places I particularly wanted to see. At least one other member of the party did the same; I met him several times in the town during this siesta time.

One of my favourite buildings was the little Ismael Samani Mausoleum, with its intricate brickwork, both inside and out, near the reservoir and the city walls, which was completed in AD 905 and was the oldest Muslim monument in the city.

Ismael Samani Mausoleum, Bukhara.   *Interior of Ismael Samani Mausoleum.*

Reservoir by city walls, Bukhara.   *Chasma Ayub Mausoleum, Bukhara.*

A short walk through a park took us to a building called the Chasma Ayub Mausoleum (Spring of Job Mausoleum), built over a spring which was supposed to have appeared when Job struck his staff on the ground. Inside, it was possible to drink from the spring, but the one glass looked so filthy that none of us tried the water. Not far away was the Ark, which was originally the royal residence within a fortress, in an area occupied since the fifth century up till 1920, when much of it was destroyed by the Red Army. Several buildings inside did not fall into a complete ruin and were now museums. There was also still a mosque and, unroofed since 1920, the huge Reception and Coronation Court. Just inside the entrance were several small rooms, which were supposed to have been the cells in which Colonel Stoddart and Captain Conolly were kept in 1842 before being led out to be beheaded before a vast crowd. Behind the Ark was the Zindon, now a museum, which was a jail with a notorious pit into which, it was said, some prisoners were thrown and left with food thrown down to them until they died.

Entrance to the Ark, Bukharta.

Across the main road opposite the Ark was the Bolo Hauz Mosque, which was built in 1718 as the emir's official place of worship. This was an unusual building, as the many wooden columns were very tall and thin, and the ceiling above them and the entrance wall were brightly painted.

Bolo Hauz Mosque, Bukhara. *Typical street scene, Bukhara.*

From behind the Ark, there was a good view to a market street and another remarkable area of the old city with mosques, medressas, and the famous Kalyon minaret. There were also three small covered mini bazaars, which were originally each devoted to one trade. At my previous visit, I bought an Uzbek hat in the hatters' market, where they had been making and selling hats for hundreds of years (though some of the shops were now selling other objects as well). This also was the area where we saw a large number of craftsmen at work. On a little side street, I visited an active mosque which, though needing some tender loving care, still had some very old mosaic work and an alarmingly antiquated central heating system, with a very thick rusty pipe to remove fumes to the outside.

Kalyon Minaret, Bukhara.

Street craftsmen, Bukhara.

There were also several other places that we took the coach to visit. I was particularly pleased to see the Char Minar, with its four little blue domes, which was built as a gatehouse of a medressa which has long since disappeared. When I had visited before, one of the towers was under scaffolding, and I was not allowed to go near it. Now it looked much finer, and we were allowed inside, where we climbed up a stairway onto the roof below the decorative towers, which look like minarets but had no function except for the aesthetic. We also visited a nineteenth-century palace, which had been turned into a museum with an attractive display of china, including a costume room where several of the group were dressed up in original Uzbek costumes.

Char Minar, Bukhara.

Museum with china display, Bukhara.

On our final evening, we had supper in a rooftop restaurant in the old town, from where we had a fine view and also saw a lovely sunset. The next day, we set out across Kyzylkum desert, along the road towards Khiva.

Bukhara sunset.

Desert road to Khiva.

I had wanted to visit Khiva for a long time. The road was mainly flat and dreary through sandy countryside with little of interest, except for the occasional tent belonging to some nomad family. As we came nearer to the city, the land became greener, and we crossed the Amu Darya River. Once we reached Urgench, the last thirty-five kilometres was along a straight road lined with trees and cotton fields. Khiva itself was a small city, only about one kilometre long and a half wide, completely surrounded by high city walls, so it was possible to see it all by foot, and there was a lot to see, for it was now, in effect, a museum city, though a museum in which people do live and carry out their daily lives. Our small hotel was excellently situated just across the square outside the West Gate, so we had an excellent view of the city walls as soon as we left the front door. Many of the buildings in Khiva dated from the early nineteenth century, though it was important to remember that this was a time when people lived more like those here did in the Middle Ages. Some of the buildings were older, but nothing inside the walls was modern; it was a perfect representation of an earlier age. Immediately inside the gate, on the left-hand side, was the Ark (Fortress), built right against the city walls. There were many fine rooms inside this building, and it was also possible to climb a very steep and long staircase to the roof, from where it was possible to gain a fine all-round view of the city and out over the walls. I had just reached the top when I heard some voices from halfway down: "Oh, there is a good view from this window. I don't think I can go any further up."

"Well, Dermot's gone on up, so we jolly well ought to be able to get there too."

About half of our group made it to the top.

View of Khiva from city walls.   *City walls, Khiva.*

The view along the top of the walls gave some idea of their size, and since they continued the whole way round the city, it must make them some of the most impressive in the world, even though they were less well known than some others, such as Avila in Spain or Dogubeyazit in Turkey.

When we returned to ground level and re-entered the street, we were immediately confronted by the tiled Kalta Minor Minaret, which is another of the remarkable buildings in Khiva and unlike any minaret I have ever seen. It was unfinished, because Mohammed Amin Khan, who started building it in 1851, died suddenly in 1855. He had intended it to be so tall that he could see all the way to Bukhara, though it is unlikely that he would have succeeded in this, seeing that the distance to Bukhara is over 480 kilometres, but it would almost certainly have been the tallest building in the world at that time. However, though it was short and stubby, it was covered with the most marvellous turquoise-coloured tiles and completely dominated the street; it was difficult to imagine the effect it would have given had it been completed.

Kalta Minor Minaret, Khiva.

Even without this minaret, the street itself would have been most attractive, for there was a medressa as well as shops and several museums, one of them a music museum inside what had been an early twentieth-century medressa.

Next to the medressa was the Sayid Alauddin Mausoleum, dating from 1310; there were a number of people praying in front of the nineteenth-century tiled sarcophagus, and a number of others being given instruction by an imam. Not far away was the Juma Mosque, a little over a thousand years old but mainly rebuilt in the sixteenth century, with its roof supported by well over two hundred wooden columns, a few of which were highly decorated and dated from the time of its original building. In the middle of this, there was an area open to the sky, where some women had clothes and decorated cloth and a few other knickknacks for sale. Opposite the Juma Mosque was another medressa, now turned into a museum of nature, history, and religion, including the history of the medressa itself.

Near to this was a supermarket in an old building situated next to the long tunnel of the East Gate. The entrance to this supermarket was through a very old carved wooden door and down some steep steps. Inside, I found one of the cashiers doing her calculations on an old abacus rather than using the more modern till.

Medressa in Khiva.   *Entrance to supermarket, Khiva.*

There were a number of streets leading off from the main west-to-east street, all of them attractive and containing interesting buildings. To the north, one of the most interesting was the Tosh-Hovli Palace. It was built in the 1830s as a more comfortable place for the ruling khans to live in than the Ark. There were nine courtyards and some 150 rooms decorated with ceramic tiles, carved stone, and wood. The ceilings were also high so that any cool air could circulate. The first architect was executed for failing to complete the building in two years. In several rooms were women selling scarves, handbags, ceramics, and rugs. It was interesting that in the buildings, it tended to be women selling, and in the outdoor stalls, men were normally doing the trading.

Tosh-Hovli Palace, Khiva.

To the south from the main street stood two of Khiva's most modern Islamic buildings: the Islam Hoja Medressa and Minaret, both built in 1910 and fitting in well with the other monuments. The minaret was beautifully decorated, and at fifty-seven metres tall, it was the highest in Uzbekistan. It was possible to climb up inside this minaret for a small charge, but one of the men in our group was at first refused entry as being too old (although he was some ten years younger than me). He was eventually allowed up when his wife paid a large deposit in case he had to be carried down; she said that she would take responsibility should he have an accident. In view of his troubles over entry, I did not try to go up, and indeed he was the only member of our group who did make the ascent, encountering no difficulties either up or down.

Islam Hoja Minaret, Khiva.

In view of the heat, our tour was taken in the morning, and after lunch in an open air restaurant, we were free to do as we wished. I decided to forgo my siesta and continue exploring the town. In one building, which was a sort of museum of native crafts, there were a number of people weaving rugs and demonstrating the art of embroidery. Everywhere there was tourist memorabilia for sale, though there were few tourists to buy.

Weavers in Khiva.

Walking through the streets was fascinating. There was one place by the North Gate where it was possible to climb up a steep bank to the top of the walls, but there was no possibility of walking along the top. Not far away, there was a fine mosque, which I could not enter because it was undergoing what looked like a very great restoration. My most interesting discovery was the burial ground in the south-western corner of the city, where hundreds of old stone tombs were crammed together right against the old walls.

Mosque restoration, Khiva.

Burial ground, Khiva.

I found Khiva the finest city I had seen in the country, even beating Bukhara, and possibly the most beautiful town I had ever seen anywhere in the world, because it was such a complete entity, with nothing inside the walls to spoil it in any way. There were only a few new buildings outside the walls, and those were not of a sort to detract from what was inside.

We flew back to the capital from Urgench, flying fairly low so that we could see clearly how the desert ended in a sharp line as we approached Tashkent. This was the end of a fascinating holiday, which improved with every place we visited.

Islam Hoja Medressa and Minaret, Khiva.

Khiva view.

C H A P T E R 5

NORTHEAST TURKEY: TRABZON TO ERZURUM

Osk Vank Church, near Lake Tortum.

Since the beginning of 2009, I had taken three tours and had one family holiday abroad. I now wanted to revisit the north-eastern part of Turkey but could not find any tour which took in all the places I wished to see, so I decided to try a tailor-made holiday. I carefully worked out all the places I wanted to stay at, decided how many nights I should stay at each place, and even suggested the actual hotels that might be suitable. I then went to my local travel agent, Bath Travel in Sherborne, to see if they could find someone who could arrange this trip, with a car and an English-speaking driver. Had I known the way the roads had improved since my last trip there, some ten years before, I would have just said what I wanted to see and left the actual itinerary to them. Bath Travel found Anatolian Sky for me, who arranged everything, even including all the hotels that I had suggested (except for the one at Erzurum).

I had decided to start with three nights in Istanbul, once again at the Hotel Avicenna. I mainly saw my favourite sights. One place I went to that I had not seen for many years was the Valide Hani, just below the Grand Bazaar. On my previous visit, many of the hundreds of rooms were being used for rug making; the clicking noise of the looms could be heard from a distance, and much of the roof was covered by rugs laid out to dry, though part of the roof was occupied by a sheep. Now, however, most of the rooms seemed to be unoccupied, with only a few being used as offices; weeds were growing out of the roof, with only a couple of rugs laid out, and the whole place seemed very dilapidated. In the Yerebatan Saray Cistern, on the other hand, new and more colourful lighting seemed to have been installed, which showed up the columns more clearly (albeit in a rather vivid colour).

Valide Hani, Istanbul.
Yerebatan Saray Cistern, Istanbul.

When I visited St Sophia this time, I found I could get better views than before, because there was less scaffolding. When the repairs to the building were started, the scaffolding had been of wood, but for many years now, it has been tubular metal. I had a pleasant surprise when I went to the Topkapi Palace, for I found that the Janissaries Band was giving a performance. I had previously seen them twice at the Military Museum and also on two separate occasions when they had appeared outside the Dome Hotel in Kyrenia, to celebrate the National Day of the Turkish Republic of Northern Cyprus. On one of these occasions, I had managed to talk with a few of the members of the band, who spoke some English. I recognised several of the performers on this occasion. Once again, I found myself thinking how terrifying their noise must have been to an enemy when it led an army into battle.

St Sophia, Istanbul.

Janisseries Band in the Topkapi Palace, Istanbul.

After my stay in Istanbul, I flew to Trabzon, where I was met by my driver, Murat, and transported to my hotel. I found I had struck lucky, for he proved to be a very good driver; he spoke good English and, to my great surprise, ran his own travel agency on the south coast of Turkey. Apparently, he had come himself instead of sending one of his drivers so he could learn more about the northeast of the country and instruct his drivers if they had to bring people to this area.

I had stayed in this hotel several times in the past but found that in the nearly ten years since I had been there, it had increased in size and comfort. In particular, the downstairs restaurant had disappeared, and instead, there was a top-floor restaurant with the most wonderful views in every direction through large glass windows.

St Sophia, Trabzon.   *Fresco in St Sophia, Trabzon.*

The next day, we went first to visit the Trabzon St Sophia. The word "Sophia" in fact means "Holy Wisdom", so both it and the one in Istanbul should really be called the "Church of Holy Wisdom". When we arrived, the church was very full, with visitors from a cruise ship, but they soon left (probably to see the famous ruined monastery of Sumela in its extraordinary cliff face position), and we had St Sophia almost to ourselves. I was able to spend as long as I wished looking at the wonderful frescos.

I had decided not to see Sumela this time, since I had seen it four times before, but instead went to see the monastery at Vazelon, far less well preserved and more difficult to find. I had visited it only once before, in the rain, and I was keen to see it again and in particular to find out if the frescos in the little roofless side chapel had survived. The track up towards the building had deteriorated considerably since my previous visit, and on several occasions, the bottom of our car was badly scraped by the rough ground; Murat muttered that if he had to come again, he would have a four-wheel-drive vehicle. At last we arrived in sight of the building in its steep wooded position and reached the muddy, slippery footpath, which led towards the monastery. I had covered about three-quarters of the way when I reached a place where a landslide had destroyed the path. There was no way across, so I had to return to the parked car and be content with the view from a distance.

Vazelon Monastery, near Trabzon.

We now returned to the main road, had lunch in a café in a small town, and (after a repair to the underside of the car) returned towards Trabzon. On the way, we turned off the main road and drove up a steep track to see the monastery of Kaymakli. I had visited this building on several occasions in the past, always approaching it from above, but Murat decided that this would be an easier way, and so it proved.

Kaymakli Monastery had been turned into a farm, and the monastery church was now a barn. I had never before been able to see the frescos as a whole, because different sections of the wall had always been hidden by piles of hay and agricultural implements. On my first visit, two youths who had been instructed by their elders to show us the way down had never seen inside the barn before and were fascinated, both by the wall paintings and the fact that they found a hen sitting on some eggs on a windowsill. Since my last visit, a new corrugated iron roof had been installed, and when the farmer's son appeared with a key, I went inside to find the barn completely empty, so that all the frescos were visible in their full glory (though the light was not good because the windows had been filled with stones, presumably to protect the interior from the elements). However, I gained the impression that someone had woken up to the fact that the frescos, covering all the walls, were a national treasure and in need of protection.

Kaymakli Monastery, Trabzon.   *Fresco in Kaymakli Monastery, Trabzon.*

Trabzon itself was now a modern city and port. The park near the hotel had been covered by open air cafés, and the main road along the coast was an up-to-date four-lane highway, clogged with heavy traffic, as was a parallel road higher up the hill. There were still a number of places of interest to be found in the city. One of these was a small museum whose rooms were in an old mansion and furnished to show what life for a rich family would have been like in the nineteenth century. Near the museum was a little old church, with men sitting outside playing cards and backgammon. The church itself was firmly shut and locked; the padlock looked as if it had not been opened for a very long time, but there were still some external carvings above a doorway. Near to the church, there was an old bazaar area with narrow, windy streets and small shops, full of locals doing their shopping (unlike the nearly empty modern stores in a nearby pedestrian shopping area).

A steep gorge, with an attractive bridge crossing halfway down the sides, led to the remains of the city walls, which completely enclosed the old part of the city on a narrow hill, though there was not much left of the fabled "Towers of Trebizond". Inside the walls, I discovered a large building which used to be a church and was now a mosque, a reminder that Trabzon had remained an independent Christian Byzantine state for some fifteen years after the fall of Constantinople to the Turks in 1453.

Trabzon Museum.

Trabzon locked church.

Trabzon church, now an active mosque.

The next day, we set off for Artvin. The first time I had driven from Trabzon to Artvin, the road had been very poor, and we had had to spend a night at Hopa before driving on to Artvin the next morning. Even the last time I had driven the road, it had taken the best part of a day. Now the road was a dual carriageway as far as Hopa, where we turned inland and took a brand-new road running high above a new reservoir. There was very little traffic on the road once we had left the environs of Trabzon, with the result that we reached Artvin in under three hours: plenty of time for me to walk out into the town and find some lunch in a typical Turkish café, where several tables were occupied by old men playing backgammon and drinking beer.

The town of Artvin started down in a deep valley and then climbed steeply for hundreds of feet. The Hotel Karahan was in the main town, high up with wonderful views. When we booked in at the desk, the man at the reception said, "Oh, my uncle [Mr Karahan] saw your name on the list yesterday and said that you were an old friend." This was rather startling to me, since the last time I had stayed at the hotel had been some ten years earlier (though Jacynth and I had stayed there several times before that). When we had first stayed there, it had been described in a guide book as being a surprisingly good hotel in the east of Turkey, and it was a place where ambassadors and archaeologists were accustomed to staying. Mr Karahan himself had built the hotel; he was the first person to realise the importance of the Georgian church buildings in the Pontic Mountains and started a movement to save them or their ruins. He then set about building a motel in Kars for the tours which were expected to be arriving to visit the old Armenian capital of Ani. Unfortunately, before the building was completed, the Kurdish troubles in the area exploded; no new tours arrived, and even the tours which had been coming disappeared, so he was nearly bankrupted. The last time we stayed there, his Kars motel had become, in effect, a bordello for long-distance lorry drivers, and for a time a part of the Hotel Karahan itself was turned over to Russian "Natashas", as the girls were called. But even though the Natashas had now gone, the hotel had never fully recovered.

Mr Karahan himself was now over ninety and had just returned from a triple heart bypass; he spent much of his time sleeping. Unfortunately, he insisted on keeping full control instead of allowing his nephew any real say in the organisation, so the whole place had gone downhill. I found myself wondering what its future would be. I recently spoke to someone who stayed there a year after this; the hotel had gone further downhill, though there was no other proper hotel in the town.

The view from the hotel now included the huge excavations for a new reservoir in the valley on the road farther south. My window looked out over a small park and playground. I was horrified to see that due to some building work below, there was a sheer drop of some thirty feet from the edge of the playground, with no protective fencing or wall. Small children were still playing there. This visit had hit the time of the Artvin festival, and while the main site of the activities, including bull fighting, was several miles farther up in the mountains, there were a number of musical and dancing events taking place in the streets of the town itself.

Artvin festival.   *Artvin festival.*   *Artvin café*

View from Hotel Karahan, Artvin.   *Children's playground, Artvin.*

We spent enough time in Artvin for me to be able to walk around quite a lot of the upper town; we also drove out to see several of the Georgian churches. The first of these was Dolishane Church, the nearest of these buildings to Artvin. Jacynth and I had visited it on our first trip to this area. Then the road had been horrific, for when we had turned off the so-called main road, we had had to drive for about five kilometres up a very rough, steep, and windy narrow track, with a cliff rising above us on one side and dropping down equally steeply on the other. There had been no vegetation at all until we reached the green oasis of the tiny scattered village. The church at that time had had a floor inserted halfway up. While the top floor had been serving as a mosque, the ground floor was being used as storage for agricultural instruments. Now everything had changed. The main road was well surfaced and ran along much higher, above where the new reservoir was being built, and the side road, much shorter since it started so much higher, had been widened, and the surface was more stabilised (except for the last steep cobbled track up to the church).

The church itself had also been much changed. A new small mosque had been built nearby, the upper floor in the church had been removed, and the whole building left empty. The local imam told me that the whole village took part in emergency repairs, and they welcomed visitors. Despite the very small numbers of villagers, they were obviously very proud of this building and pleased that people from other countries might come and see it. There were even plans to build a small café to welcome coach parties. One thing which had not been changed was the ancient wooden ladder on the outside, leading from the roof to the dome; it looked as if it had not been touched for over a hundred years. I would not like to have climbed it.

Dolishane Church.   *Dolishane Church.*   *View from Dolishane.*

Our next journey was to drive farther south to see the area round Yusufeli. To reach that area, we drove past the turn to Dolishane and down into the valley to where the road split; the left hand went to Kars, and the right, which we took, went up the valley of the River Coruh towards Erzurum. The road here was worse than we had expected, for it had been decided many years before to turn this long valley into yet another reservoir, and a new road was being built well above where the waterline would be. Soon after passing the Dolishane turn, we passed a large viaduct which was being built to accommodate the new road. The present road was not, in the meantime, being kept in good repair, and as we drove up the valley, we saw that most of the houses were already deserted. At one point, the road was closed for half an hour while debris from the new construction above was thrown down and had to be cleared. Exactly the same happened on our return journey.

Viaduct in building.

Road works towards Yusufeli.

The first place we went to see was Ishan. This, like Dolishane, was a little village set in a small, lush green oasis after a climb up a steep hill in a very bleak mountain setting. Here was a much larger church than Dolishane, set on a wide flat area, one side of which was very marshy; the other had been levelled into a playground for children from the small local school. Unlike my previous visits, there was no sign of any children this time. Although the main nave was roofless, it had a very fine dome, and the faded remains of some frescos could be discerned on the walls and inside the dome itself.

Ishan Church near Yusufeli.

View from Ishan.

Road to Ishan.

When we left Ishan, we drove to the village of Yusufeli. In the 1970s, it was decided to build several new reservoirs along the River Coruh; the highest of these would bury the village under the waters, so for many years, there was no new building or even repairs. A few years ago, some of the villagers concluded that nothing was ever going to happen, and a few new houses were built and many repairs have taken place. This was the sign for the authorities to start building the new road, and work is likely to start on the new dam in the next few years, after the Artvin dam has been completed. After lunch on a terrace overlooking the Cayi River, we started along the lovely but unmade-up road towards Barhal, which has one of the best-preserved Georgian churches in the area; it was still used as the village mosque. I was interested to see if access to the church was now any easier, since on my last visit, one had to climb a steep rough track by a waterfall. There were a few hamlets on the other side of the river from the road, and supplies to these were delivered by means of a rope pulley. How the inhabitants reached their homes, I never discovered. I certainly would not have liked to trust myself to one of those pulleys.

Pulley access to village on road to Barhal.

We drove the twenty or so kilometres to the village of Sarigol, from where we had another ten kilometres of what I remembered as an appallingly narrow road, with a cliff up on one side and a steep drop to the other. To our surprise, we found ourselves on a fine new concrete surface. Unfortunately, some way farther on, the road was completely closed by liquid concrete being laid the full width of the track. There had been no warning signs at all. I discovered afterwards that anyone travelling to Barhal at that time had to take a taxi as far as the road works, dismount, walk some way on a muddy footpath and then meet a prearranged vehicle on the other side. We had to turn round and drive back the way we had come, and it was now too late to attempt to reach any of the other churches in the area, so we made the return trip to Artvin. This was my big disappointment of the whole tour, but I have found in many visits to Turkey that one is unusually lucky if everything goes to plan.

The road from Artvin to Kars up through the mountains and alongside Lake Cildir was beautiful, though possibly not quite as beautiful as driving downhill in the other direction, with finer views. Due to road improvements, the drive took a lot less time than when I had previously driven this route, and we arrived in time for lunch, even though we took a detour to see the ruined church of Tbeti. This was even more of a ruin than the last time I had visited, but it was still impressive in spite of the weeds, brambles, and nettles that filled its interior. I remembered the two youths who had appeared the last time Jacynth and I had been there and who had written us a very nice letter, thanking us, after we sent them copies of photographs we had taken of them.

Kars itself was a town that had improved considerably since the first time we visited; our hotel was very reasonable. I took a long walk round the town, near to the castle, and was rewarded by finding the Church of the Holy Apostles open, so that for the first time, I was able to see the attractive interior. This building was built as a church and then became a mosque and a museum before being reconsecrated as the Cumbet Mosque in 1998.

Ruins of Tbeti Church.    *Church of the Holy Apostles, Kars.*

The whole area round the castle and bridge over the river was attractive, with some old ruined buildings which, with a little restoration, could make a most pleasant area. Also on the hill nearer to the centre were a number of nineteenth-century Russian houses, which were still in good condition. The next day after our return from Ani, I walked to the museum, where I was the only visitor. This was the building where we had had to go in order to obtain our visas to visit Ani before taking them on to the police station to be stamped. It was good to find that this formality was no longer required. On my way out of the museum, the officials insisted on giving me, gratis, a CD of Kars and Ani and several postcards of the area.

The main reason for visiting Kars was to see the ruins of the old Armenian capital of Ani. The huge site of Ani is on the edge of a gorge overlooking a river, which marks the frontier of present-day Armenia. Photography was now allowed, except in the area of the citadel, where entry was still forbidden. The first time we visited, we had to deposit our cameras at a military post halfway from Kars and then wait outside the walls for an armed soldier to accompany us round.

The road to Ani, thirty-nine kilometres, according to the signpost, used to be a narrow potholed way leading through a poverty-stricken village round a forbidding-looking black pond. The new road was a fine four-lane highway, bypassing the village and leading directly to the site. On the way, we met just two tractors, and on our return, again two tractors, and this time two white mini vans, probably taking supplies to the nearby military barracks. During the whole time I was walking around the site, I encountered one group of about a dozen Turks and a group of six university students from Istanbul, one of whom was English. Shortly after our return from our previous visit some ten years previously, Jacynth and I were amused to read in the travel supplement of a newspaper a report of the writer's recent visit to eastern Turkey. He wrote that Ani was a magical place and marvelled that so few people visited it, saying that when he went, there was only a small group of Russians and an elderly English couple visiting. We remembered a Russian group, and from the dates decided we were the elderly couple mentioned. In any case, the new road had not yet brought a flood of tourists.

City walls, Ani.

Seljuk Palace, Ani.

I started walking round in an anti-clockwise direction, since this would make my favourite place the last. After entering through the gate in the very tall and lengthy walls, dating from the tenth century, I came first to the Seljuk Palace, much restored, unlike the other buildings. Next, I reached the ruins of the Church of St Gregory of Gagic, which was built in AD 998; it must have been a very large rotunda church, but only its base remained and a large number of scattered carved remnants. My next visit was to the ruins of a building sometimes called the "Kervansaray" or the Church of the Holy Apostles. This building was further into the site, away from the edge, and in a bit of a dip. It seems to have started as a church and then had an inn added later, and it was not easy to see where one ended and the other began. Nevertheless, it was an impressive building. The little round church of St Gregory Agibhamrets, by contrast, stood on a ridge, was visible from almost anywhere on the site, and was in remarkably good condition.

The ruins of some shops, which were being excavated on my previous visit, had now been left neglected and, while still visible, were largely overgrown with vegetation. Also visible from a considerable distance was the mosque, with its unusual hexagonal-shaped minaret, which made it look rather like a factory building. However, the visit to the inside, apart from showing some fine architecture, had the most wonderful view down the gorge to the river and across the ruined bridge to Armenia.

Church of St Gregory Agibhamrets, Ani.   *View of mosque over shops, Ani.*

On the opposite side of the gorge, there used to be watch towers with armed soldiers in them. Though a few of the watch towers were still there, they now appeared to be empty. However, there was some quarrying being performed on the Armenian side, and the Turks claimed that the vibrations were causing damage to the buildings left in Ani.

View from Ani Mosque.   *View from Ani Mosque.*   *Church of the Redeemer, Ani.*

Personally, I doubted whether the quarrying had anything to do with the damage. Half of the Church of the Redeemer collapsed in 1957 as the result of a lightning strike, and other buildings had deteriorated over the years due to neglect, added to which there may well have been earthquake tremors, for the whole of Turkey is in the danger zone and often suffers. However, since my last visit, the authorities had shored up several buildings with ugly red metal tubing to stop further collapse. This temporary repair included the cathedral, which had been missing its dome for centuries.

The Cathedral, Ani.   *The Cathedral, Ani.*

My favourite building was the church of Tigran Honents, which was situated halfway down the gorge and whose inside walls were covered with the finest frescos. I was horrified on this visit to find that one section of wall, which had held some of the best frescos, was now bare. I could not discover whether the frescos had been stolen or carried off to some museum or merely collapsed. There was, however, now a guardian there, keeping an eye on all visitors and also selling drinking water. The walk around Ani took me about three hours, which I gathered was about average.

Church of Tigran Honents, Ani, with frescos.

The next day, we drove to Erzurum, where we arrived in time for lunch. The hotel proved to be very comfortable and was situated right in the centre. This had as one advantage only a very short walk to the jewellery shops, situated in the sixteenth-century Rustem Pasa Bedestan, where in the nineteenth century, thousands of laden camels and traders used to stay every year. It was now almost entirely devoted to items made from the obsidian-like stone found nearby, and I was able to buy some unusual necklaces as presents for members of my family.

Rustem Pasa Bedestan, Erzurum.   *Inside Rustum Pasa Bedestan.*

The next day, we drove along the road to the north, near Tortum Lake, and turned off to drive up the track to Osk Vank Church, my personal favourite among the Georgian churches in Turkey. It was kept in fair condition for a time when it was being used as a mosque (indeed, the locals still call it "the Old Mosque"), but now greenery sprouted from its roof and large cracks appeared in some of the walls, though a few frescoes remained, and many carvings were still in good condition.

Osk Vank Church, near Tortum Lake.

As had been the case in all my previous visits to this church, there was no one else there except for a few locals. As I have said before, this was not a tourist area.

Our next visit was not very far away but much more difficult to find. Haho Church (Khakhuli) had, until recently, remained in good condition, because it had been used as a mosque since the sixteenth century. This was the monastery where the magnificent

Khakhuli Triptych was made (it is now in the Icon Museum in Tbilisi, Georgia). I had only been inside once and was hoping I might do so again, for there was some fine carving on some of the columns there. Unfortunately, not only was the place locked, but from the little that was visible through the windows, it looked as though it was unused and falling into disrepair. It was even difficult to obtain a good view of the fine carved eagle, above the windows beneath the dome, since a tree was growing up and blocking the view from many angles.

Khakhuli Church, near Tortum Lake.

While we were there, two men appeared, carrying clipboards. They spoke no English but told Murat that they were part of a government-funded organisation which was examining historic buildings in the area to see that they were all being looked after and to make sure that repairs were made when necessary; they said that something urgent was needed in this case. I hope their report will save this building, but I am not holding my breath.

After this trip, I had the next day free in Erzurum and was able to explore the city. Much reconstruction was going on. The whole of what had been a green park off the main street had been dug up; it had contained benches and made an attractive surrounding for the elaborately carved twelfth-century Yakutiye Medressa, which holds a Museum of Islamic and Turkish Art, and the Lala Mustafa Pasa Mosque. The medressa was also under restoration and closed, so I was not able to see the beautiful interior, though the mosque was still open. I hope a new garden is planted in this large area and there are no new buildings erected.

*Lala Mustafa Pasa Mosque and
Yakutiye Medressa, Erzurum.*

Minaret of Yakutiye Medressa.

Luckily, farther down the main street, the Old Mosque and the best known of Erzurum's monuments, the Cifte Minareli Medressa, were not being restored and were open to view as usual.

Cifte Minareli Medressa, Erzurum.

There were also many other places of interest within walking distance but away from the main street. I was able to visit the citadel, where I had not been before, and the Archaeological Museum, in which I was the only visitor. How some of these Turkish museums exist I do not know, for even in Istanbul, they were never crowded, and yet they had marvellous exhibits. I suppose it may be that there are so many things to see in Turkey that people who visit only once or twice just rush to the best known and to those within reaching distance of cruise ships. Places such as Erzurum and Kars are only really reachable in the summer months, since they are at nearly 2,000 metres and are covered in deep snow all the winter.

Another delightful place I visited was the Uc Kumbetler, a group of three attractive mausoleums situated not far behind the Cifte Minareli. Like many of the monuments in Erzurum, they are surrounded by mainly modern buildings, for most of the old houses were being pulled down and replaced by uglier but doubtlessly far more comfortable and warmer new blocks.

The Old Mosque, Erzurum.

Uc Kumbetler Mausolea, Erzurum.

From Erzurum, we drove back to Trabzon, stopping only to pick up a few pieces of the local black stone from an embankment on the way. I then flew back to Heathrow via Istanbul, after another most interesting and enjoyable holiday.

The dome, Ishan Church near Yusufeli.

CHAPTER 6

WARSAW AND THE CHOPIN ANNIVERSARY

The Castle Square and Column of Sigismund III, Warsaw.

My last holiday for 2010 was to be something entirely different. I had decided to take my seventeen-year-old grandson with me. David was about to start his final year at school, where he was studying physics and mathematics; he is also a very keen musician. He has now obtained the Royal School of Music Grade Eight in Keyboard Playing and Singing as well as being a skilful composer, and I knew that something with music involved would be very much to his taste. I had originally thought of taking him to Prague, a lovely city where it is always possible to find musical performances of one sort or another happening. By pure chance, I spotted a musical tour run by Kirker Holidays to coincide with the Polish celebrations of the two hundredth anniversary of the birth of Chopin. It was conveniently dated to return a couple of days before the start of his term. David agreed with this idea, so we booked to go to Warsaw, a city I had never visited before. It was to be an excellent choice. There were five scheduled concerts as well as visits to many of the places connected with Chopin. I am no musician myself but very much enjoyed listening to classical music, as did the majority of our group of nine plus the manager. David, in spite of being far and away the youngest (the manager was in his late forties or early fifties, and the next youngest in the group was sixty-four), probably knew more about music than any of us except for the manager. Luckily, his youth did not worry anyone, and we all got on very well together.

The Royal Palace, Warsaw, with memorials to the dead President.

Our hotel, the Bristol, proved to be in a very good position on the Royal Route, next door to the Presidential Palace. Only a few weeks before, the president and several members of his government had been killed in a plane crash on a visit to Russia. A simple wooden cross had been erected in front of the palace as a memorial, and flowers and other mementos were laid on the other side of the main road. We were told that there was an ongoing row about this memorial, some people saying that it was unsuitable and that it should be removed, while others felt so strongly that it should remain that there were always a number of them on guard, some of them sleeping there overnight, to make sure that the cross was not removed. There were also police stationed there to make sure there was no trouble between the different factions. The matter was resolved peaceably some weeks later, and the cross was removed to a different, more suitable, place where it could remain safely.

Our first visit was to the Baroque Church of Visitation, where Chopin had played the organ as a boy. Outside this church was a statue of the first Polish pope, John Paul II.

Church of Visitation, Warsaw.   *Statue of Pope John Paul 11.*

A little farther up the street, on the other side, was the Holy Cross Church, which contains the pillar in which Chopin's heart is buried (it was brought back from Paris by his sister), and near to that, opposite the entrance of the university, which we did not visit, was the Chopin Museum in the Ostrogoski Palace, containing a lot of the composer's memorabilia, including a piano on which he was supposed to have played.

Chopin Memorial in Holy Cross Church.   *Chopin Museum in Ostrogoski Palace.*

One day, we were driven out a number of miles from Warsaw to a village called Zelazowa Wola, which was where Chopin was born. The house itself was not large but was in the centre of a large garden with a stream running through it, and several busts of the composer were scattered around. There was also a small museum and shop and a café just inside the entrance to the garden. While we were here, we had an unexpected treat, for there was to be a piano recital. Benches were laid out on one side of the house, where a double door was opened so we could hear the pianist playing on the same sort of piano that Chopin had used. It was possible to hear the music clearly from these seats and also from many other parts of the garden to which the music was broadcast. Most of the time, we sat in warm sunshine, and not even a sudden heavy shower could spoil the occasion.

Zelazowa Wola, Chopin's birthplace, with statues of Chopin.

Not all of our visits were to places connected with Chopin. We visited the Royal Lazienski Park and the Palace on the Water, as it is commonly called. Unfortunately, it was raining hard at the time of our visit, so we contented ourselves with visiting the building and viewing the rain-sodden park from the palace itself. However, this building was well worth the visit. We were rather startled when we went inside and bought the entrance tickets, for we were told to take off our shoes and don some large felt slippers. However, no sooner had I started bending down to shed my shoes than the militaristic-looking guard came over, stopped me, and waved me through. There are some advantages in looking ancient!

The rooms were very well laid out and furnished in eighteenth—and nineteenth-century styles. It was originally a seventeenth-century bath house but was later remodelled to serve as a summer residence for the kings of Poland. Some of the floors were made of lovely patterned inlaid wood, and it was possible to see why most visitors were not allowed to wear their normal shoes. Some seventeenth-century bas-reliefs survived in the original bathroom, as did the fine Delft tiles which lined the walls. Many of the ceilings in the state rooms were finely painted in a baroque style.

In the park stood the best-known statue of Chopin, sitting under a weeping willow tree. Concerts were frequently performed in front of this statue, though none were while we were in Warsaw (the weather would not have made for a pleasant experience). In fact, the weather in general was not at all settled during the whole of our visit, though there were a few sunny and warmer patches.

We also stopped for chocolate and cakes in another of the buildings in the park. This was a frequent and welcome type of repast during a mid-morning break.

The Palace on the Water, Lazienski Park, Warsaw.

We did take one full day trip, away from Warsaw, to Cracow. For this journey, we travelled by train. I had been particularly looking forward to this visit, since I had loved the city when Jacynth and I had been there some years previously. The scenery for much of the journey was very flat and uninteresting. We started in rain, and though the weather improved for a part of the journey, as we approached the hilly area around Cracow, it started again in earnest just as we arrived. It is not only British trains which run behind time, for we arrived over an hour late, to our great annoyance, for our time in Cracow was to be limited. We could not take a later train back to Warsaw if we were to be in time for our evening concert.

At the entrance to the station, there was someone taking advantage of the weather by selling umbrellas, and several of our group, including David, used this service. I did not need to, for I had my small collapsible umbrella with me.

The station was only a short distance from the city walls, and we entered through a gate near where local artists hang their pictures. Because of the weather, there were few pictures on display. We walked through the Market Square, possibly the largest city square in medieval Europe, but did not visit the old Cloth Hall in its centre, with many shops selling amber and other jewellery. Instead, we made straight for Jagiellan University off the far end of the square. Jacynth and I had been through the entrance gates but not round the building. We then had to wait for some time for the English-speaking guide to appear, for she had been expecting us an hour earlier. The tour of the university was interesting and held, among other things, some early scientific instruments and some busts of Louis XVI and Marie Antoinette of France.

Jagiellan University, Cracow.

By the time we had finished our tour, the rain had decreased to a drizzle, so we took a short walk through an old part of the city; we found a place from where we could see the castle hill, though we did not have time to climb it. I had also asked if it would be possible to see the famous Leonardo da Vinci painting *Lady with an Ermine* but was told it was away at an exhibition elsewhere. We lunched in a pleasant café, that I had visited on my previous trip; it overlooked the square, and it was possible to hear the famous bugle call which takes place every hour day and night, from the top of St Mary's Church, in memory of a bugler who seven hundred years ago gave warning of a Tartar attack. He was shot in the neck by an arrow, and this was shown in the music, which ended suddenly in the middle of a note. We then had to leave to catch our return train.

The five concerts we attended in Warsaw took place in different venues, most of which we were able to reach on foot from our hotel. We did have to take our coach to the concert held in the Television Centre, and when it tried to enter by the wrong entrance, it was turned away, as were a large number of other vehicles all making the same mistake. The man at the wrong gate was obviously fed up with the number of times he had to instruct people where to go. All the concerts were of a high standard, and David and I enjoyed them very much.

The Bristol Hotel, besides being in a most convenient position for the concerts, was also the most famous hotel in Poland; in 1997, it was ranked number 38 in the top 100 hotels in the world. The lobby had hundreds of small brass plaques with the names of famous world figures who had stayed there, including Margaret Thatcher (who attended the reopening after its renovation in 1993), Prince Philip (who stayed at least three times), and the Rolling Stones.

The Bristol Hotel, Warsaw.

Another place we visited was the large landscaped garden of Wilanow Palace, on the outskirts of Warsaw. This very fine palace was built towards the end of the seventeenth century as a summer retreat for King John Sobieski III and was later converted into a large palace. It now contains a museum of interiors showing a number of well-preserved rooms as well as the Polish Portrait Gallery. I found these portraits most interesting, for while British portraits were usually painted to flatter the sitter, these Polish portraits were painted to show, as Cromwell would have put it, warts and all (with an emphasis on the warts). I showed photos of some of them to the manager of Montacute House, where there were a lot of British portraits, and she nearly fell off her chair with laughter. There was filming going on while we were there, and the actors and actresses looked far more attractive than many of the portraits.

Portraits in the Wilanow Palace, Warsaw.

Wilanow Palace, Warsaw.

There was a considerable amount of time free for us to explore the city by ourselves. We were lucky in that on one of our first individual outings, we spotted a restaurant which stayed open late; it was only a five-minute walk from the hotel, so we were able to have a good meal after the evening concerts were over, and since the food was excellent, several of us walked down there regularly.

Warsaw itself was an extraordinary city, for the centre was completely destroyed during the Second World War, and both the Old Town and the New Town, which itself dated from the sixteenth century, were completely rebuilt with the aid of photographs and paintings (including several by Canaletto) to look as it had before the war. The result was that it had the feel of a medieval middle European town, though most of the houses were up-to-date inside.

Near the hotel was a park where we found the tomb to the unknown soldier; we were able to look inside but not to enter, since it was undergoing repairs. The two sentries on duty inside stood so motionless I wondered if they were waxworks; it was only at the changing of the guard that I realised they were real men.

Our way to the Old Town and the New Town was down the Royal Route, which runs the whole way from Wilanow to the New Town, and the Bristol Hotel was on this road. At the square by the start of the Old Town stood the Royal Castle, which had photographs of Warsaw before, during, and after the war.

Photo of Warsaw just after the war.   *The Royal Castle, Warsaw.*

This was a most attractive walk past many attractive churches, museums, and other interesting buildings, as well as into market squares. Much of the walk was restricted to pedestrians, occasional buses, and taxis. At one point, I passed a bride with some of her attendants sitting on a bench, obviously hoping that her transport would soon arrive before the threatening rain. There were a number of long benches along this route, each with a local map engraved in it, as well as a button which when pressed played some Chopin piano music.

The entry to the so-called New Town was through the Barbican, a building in the middle of the city walls. In the New Town, where the architecture was similar to the Old Town, we found the hotel we had been originally scheduled to use. While not as imposing as the Bristol, it too was very pleasant and in a lovely street, from the end of which there was a good view down to the Vistula River, and I would have been very happy to have stayed there had it not been for the greater distance from the concert venues. Three of us actually entered and had some delicious hot chocolate there in another luxurious lounge. One of the bridges across had on its parapet a fine statue of Syrena (or the Warsaw Mermaid, as she is usually known). Indeed, there were several statues of Syrena scattered throughout the city, which is a place noted for its statues.

Away from the Royal Route, many of the buildings were modern, and quite a lot of these of typical communistic concrete style, but the Royal Route area alone made Warsaw a city well worth a visit.

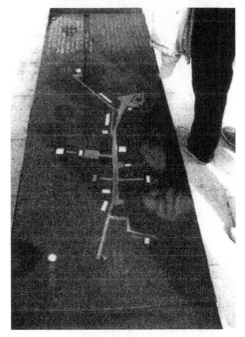

Scenes on the Royal Route.

A statue of Chopin.

Picture above the altar, Church of the Holy Cross, Warsaw.

CHAPTER 7

IRAN: LAND OF THE AYATOLLAH

Persepolis, Iran.

"Is it safe?" was the question I was almost invariably asked by people when they heard I was travelling on a tour to Iran in the spring of 2011. As it turned out, it felt as safe as any country I have travelled in, except for when I wanted to cross a city street, for the standard of driving was worse than any country I have visited, even Lebanon. A few months later, our embassy was attacked by a mob and our ambassador withdrawn, but at the time of my visit, we could not have received a more friendly welcome.

However, that is not to say I did not have any difficulties. These started in England, when it came to obtaining my visa. Cox and Kings, the tour operators, had told me I had to go up to the Iranian embassy in person to give my fingerprints. They also said they would give me a number to put on the form. They told me that one could not make an appointment but had to just turn up, and to do that when the embassy opened in the morning, when I would be given a time to appear in the afternoon. I spent a night in London and was there for the opening, together with a dozen or so Iranians. When we were given our forms, we found we were told on them to come back in nine days' time. There was nearly a riot, but one of the officials drew me aside into another room and said that if I came back between

2.30 and 3.00, they would fit me in, since I was an old man, but I was not to let the others know as I left. Age can indeed have its advantages!

The situation of Tehran, the capital, was superb, with tall snow-covered mountains rising nearby. The same cannot be said of the city itself, with its modern drab buildings and fume-ridden streets. Luckily, our hotel, the Laleh, was very acceptable, and there was a large park behind it.

After a morning's rest to recover from our flight, our party of about a dozen was driven out to see the sights; the only notable one was the Freedom Monument, a vast concrete monstrosity.

View of Tehran from Hotel Laleh.

The Freedom Monument, Tehran.

We were then taken to the National Museum of Iran in a pleasant brick building, the vaulted entrance of which was designed to look like the famous Sasamid hall in Ctesiphon, in Iraq. The labelling of the pre-Islamic collections left a lot to be desired, but all was explained by our Iranian guide, who was also our tour manager, and certainly gave me a desire to reach the sites we were to see later. After this visit, we were taken to see the National Jewels Museum in the same complex. To enter, we had to go through no less than three x-ray machines and to deposit anything metallic at the counter. While I was waiting for some of our party, I was told to move, since I was standing in the way of the sliding security doors, which would crash shut if any major alarm sounded, trapping any miscreant inside. When we finally entered, we found that all the exhibits were protected by bars in front of the cases, which were liable to set off an alarm if they were so much as touched. Indeed, the alarm went off several times during our visit, at which point loud speakers warned us, in several languages, not to touch any bars. I do not think these counted as major alarms. I have never known such security anywhere. The jewels, including several crowns and the world's largest pink diamond, were remarkable, though many of them descended into the realm of vulgarity.

After this, we were driven to the Carpet Museum, not far from our hotel. Here we were to be disappointed, since we found it closed, even though we arrived well over an hour before the official closing time. Apparently, the staff had decided to go home two hours early, as they thought not enough people were coming in.

Back at the hotel, since there was some time before we were due to meet for supper, two of us decided to walk down the half mile or so to the park entrance. On the way, we saw one of the myriad of moped drivers knocked off his vehicle. Luckily, plenty of people rushed to help, and he did not seem badly injured, though his moped was seriously damaged. By a path through the park, a large number of activity areas for different sports had been laid out, and there were many benches for people to sit on. What really surprised us was the fact that, despite the strict laws about the segregation of the sexes, young people were walking around holding hands or sitting down with arms around each other, and while the laws regarding the wearing of hijabs to cover their hair were being observed, the girls were allowing the hijabs to go further and further back on their heads. Incidentally, the laws on women's dress also had to be observed by all tourists in the country.

The next day, we took an early flight to Shiraz and went to the Eram Botanical Gardens. There have been gardens here since the Saljughid Dynasty, which ran from 1037 to 1193. They have had various owners and were now run by Shiraz University. There was a school party of girls, aged about sixteen or seventeen, just inside the entrance, who took the chance of rare foreigners and rushed up to us to practise their English; then they asked to have their photographs taken with some of our group. Their teachers looked a little worried at first but, seeing that we were quite happy, allowed all of us to get on with it. These gardens were a mixture of very formal and fairly wild. As with all the gardens we were to see, roses played an important part; they were supposed to grow over a thousand different species, though it was too early in the year for us to see many of them in flower.

The Eram Botanical Gardens, Shiraz.

We spent quite a long time walking round the gardens; I met a party of schoolboys who also demanded to have their photographs taken. When we left, we walked down the road a short way to have a good lunch in a small attractive restaurant nearby. No alcohol was served anywhere in Iran, but it was here that I discovered a non-alcoholic beer, which was very refreshing and tasted not unlike a lager. Most of the rest of the visit, I varied between this drink and bottled water, for I do not like any form of colas.

After lunch, we were taken by coach to the Friday Mosque, which had a very large courtyard. The exterior of most of the buildings were covered with mainly blue tiles. Although a mosque had stood on the site for many years, the old mosque was destroyed in an earthquake in 1852 and rebuilt, so most of what was now visible was nineteenth century. Nevertheless, it was very attractive, and I was pleased to see the floor of the mosque was covered with individual rugs rather than one large carpet, as is now so often the case in Turkey.

The Friday Mosque, Shiraz.

We then visited the tomb of Hafiz, a poet who wrote love poems which are much admired and are supposed to have mystical meanings for the Sufis. The tomb itself was set in another garden and under a small open dome. We saw a number of people who came in, knelt, laid their hands on the stone tomb, and obviously said prayers to the dead poet. We also visited the busy covered bazaar, which was near the walls round the citadel; there were many towers made of decorated bricks, reminiscent of the brickwork to be found in Bukhara in Uzbekistan.

Tomb of Hafiz garden.   *Spices in Shiraz bazaar.*   *Citadel tower, Shiraz.*

However, quite the most fascinating place we visited in Shiraz was the mausoleum of Shah Cheragh. We were very lucky to see it, for it had been closed to all non-Muslims since 2002, when a disturbance had been caused by a foreign group, and for several years, even the courtyard had been closed. However, it was now open, though the women were made to enter by a different door, where they had to hire a chador to cover them down to their feet. The building itself dated from the fourteenth century, though earthquakes and the ravages of time meant that little of the original remained. The interior walls and dome were almost entirely covered by irregularly shaped pieces of nineteenth-century glass, causing an effect I had never seen before.

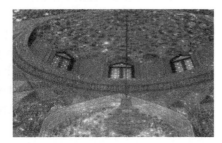

Mausoleum of Shah Cheragh, Shiraz.

Shiraz was very much a mixture of old and new. One of the very new things I saw was a multi-story car park near our hotel. It was some ten storeys high and made entirely of metal. A car would be driven into it, and the driver would dismount, and the car would be raised as though in a lift or on a big wheel. When the driver wished to reclaim his car, he would call it down and then drive it out at floor level. It certainly took up a lot less space than any other car park I have ever seen.

The next day, we went to see Persepolis. We drove out of Shiraz by the Koran Gate, which was originally built in the tenth century. It got its name from the fact that a copy of the Koran was placed in it so that anyone leaving the city by that gate would be blessed on their way. In 1950, it was demolished to allow for a new road and was rebuilt by the side of the road; we were told that it still has a copy of the Koran in it.

Shortly after leaving the city, there was a permanent police check where all vehicles had to stop. Our driver had to put on his fluorescent jacket, which he had to keep by him, and then take all his papers to an office for checking, which involved a stop of about a quarter of an hour. This check took place regularly when leaving or reaching any large town. After this, it took about an hour to reach the site itself. The car park, ticket office, and toilets were situated some considerable distance from the actual entrance to the ruins; one had to be sure to purchase entry tickets there rather than go on to the more permanent buildings by the entrance, or face a considerable walk back over the flat sandy area to purchase them. When we were there, the car park was surprisingly empty, with only a few cars and several coaches bringing schoolchildren to visit. While we were waiting near the entrance for our guide to bring the tickets, we were surrounded by school girls wanting to know all about us and demanding to have their photographs taken, while their teachers looked on mildly. Persepolis itself was such a large place that once we had climbed the steps up to the remains themselves (it stood on a huge level platform), we hardly noticed the children again.

It was quite a long flight of steps up to the site, though easy walking since the stone steps had been covered with wood to protect them from wear, except at the edges. They were very shallow steps, for when they were built in 515 BC, it was designed so that horses could be ridden up to the entrance gates. It was not in existence for very long, since Alexander razed it to the ground in 330 BC. It was ironic that though all the gold decoration was carried away, some of the bas-reliefs may have been saved by the burning, since the falling rubble probably protected them from the elements over hundreds of years.

The Great Gateway was flanked by huge statues of quadrupeds and winged bulls with human heads.

School girls at Persepolis. *Great Gateway at Persepolis.*

In the same area were several bird-headed animal capitols, which were used to support roof beams, and there was also a good view of the Hall of the 100 Columns.

Persepolis capitols. *Hall of 100 Columns, Persepolis.*

Some of the most remarkable features were the very many carved reliefs on the walls of staircases; some of those on pillars showed scenes of tribute being carried to Darius from nations that were subject to him and of servants and farm animals, as well as other scenes of life at the time. There must be literally thousands of these pictures carved in low relief in many different parts of the palace. In several places, cuneiform inscriptions could be found, some of them in several languages.

Low relief carvings in Persepolis.

I also found time to climb up a considerable hill to the Royal Tombs, cut into the rock, despite the warning from a guide book that the path was very steep and difficult. In fact, I managed it quite easily, though I saw two people having to be helped down. It was well worth the climb, for apart from the carvings on the tombs themselves, there was a fine panoramic view of the palace. We were given plenty of time to ourselves after the very instructive tour by our guide, and we spent well over three hours on the site, though even that seemed hardly enough.

After leaving Persepolis, we were driven back to the main road to see the four Achaemenid tombs carved into a cliff face high above the ground. On the way there, we passed the tents and cattle of some nomads near the side of the road.

Achaemenid tombs near Persepolis.

The tombs themselves were remarkable, especially when one realised that the ground below them had at some stage been filled in (when and for what purpose was not known) to a depth of some twenty to thirty feet. The most magnificent of the tombs held the remains of Darius the Great, who died in 486 BC. There was also a free-standing cube tower, half submerged, but now with a small area cleared around, which showed the original level of the ground. What its purpose was we do not know, for it had one door and no windows. Eventually, they may clear all the extra soil away so that it will be possible to gain a real impression of what it would have been like to see the tombs so far above the ground.

 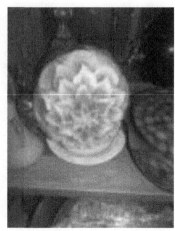

Cliff with Achaemenid tombs.　　　　　　　　*Carved melon in Shiraz.*

That evening, we had one of our best meals yet in a local restaurant, where they had displayed a melon carved into a very fancy shape; several of the group tried to guess what this fruit was.

The next day, we set out for Isfahan, and after the customary stop at the check point, we made good time along the road, until we turned off to see the tomb and the remains of the palace of Cyrus. Something rather amusing happened here. A coach arrived with a party of very attractive girls, who were students at a university. I soon had a group of half a dozen around me, wanting to find out where I lived and what I did. They discovered I was a widower, and one of them asked how old I was. When I replied that I would soon be eighty-two, she said, "Oh, you should get married again. Any one of us will marry you." I politely refused the offer.

Tomb of Cyrus and me with university students.　　*Ruins of palace of Cyrus.*

The tomb itself was fairly plain and very dignified. To judge by the remains, the palace and the audience chamber, situated several hundred yards away from the palace, must have been much more elaborate. The whole complex was situated on what was now a huge, flat, sandy and dusty plain, growing only a few weeds leading up to some hills. It was difficult to imagine that this dreary area was once, under Cyrus, a garden so magnificent that the word "paradise" is supposed to have come from it.

At one point on our journey, we were waved down by two policemen. Our driver got out, grumbling that he had not been speeding. He came back grinning and spoke to our guide, who burst out laughing. Apparently the police had been on duty there since the early hours of the morning, and they had not had any food or drink since arriving; they wondered if we had any spare food or drink in the coach. We were able to give them some water and fruit, for which they were very grateful.

At one point on the journey, we came to an area bristling with notices forbidding all photography; there were ancient-looking guns all pointing in one direction as well as a few armoured vehicles. Some miles after the start of this, there were large embankments on one side of the road, over which we could just see the tops of some roofs a little way off. Our guide told us that this was an atomic research establishment and the guns were there to protect it against any air attack. I could not think that any of the guns we saw would have been of much use against Israeli missiles.

We stopped for lunch at a large roadside restaurant, where I was not able to resist taking a photograph of an unusual sign in the grounds. We then carried on through attractive country surrounded by high hills until we reached Isfahan and the magnificent Abassi Hotel.

Sign in restaurant grounds.

Nearing Isfahan.

This hotel was undoubtedly the place to stay in Isfahan, though it was expensive (but the cost of it was covered in my tour). Normally, I am not keen on large hotels and far prefer the small and more homely places, but this was one of the exceptions. It was originally the caravanserai of the last shah's mother, and she used to put up her favoured visitors there. It was attached to some of the buildings of the Chahar Bagh Theological School, and the dome of its mosque was clearly visible from the lovely gardens and from many of its 230 rooms, suites, and apartments, which were furnished in the style of Safavid and Qajar architecture. The public rooms were also decorated luxuriously. The gardens were magnificent, and several of us sat for a long time at a café table, eating a little snack. The gardens were visible from the restaurant and from all of the rooms. At night, they were floodlit, as was the dome of the mosque. Unfortunately, we were not able to visit the mosque, which was supposed to be very beautiful inside, for it was closed for, fatal word, restoration. The hotel was also well positioned and within walking distance of the Maydan Imam Square, probably the most beautiful part of the city, though to do that walk meant risking one's life crossing two busy roads.

The Abassi Hotel, Isfahan, and its gardens.

The next morning, we started by visiting the Cehel Sotun Palace, sometimes known as the Palace of Forty Columns, situated in a vast royal park. The twenty wooden columns in the front were reflected in a rectangular pond. The entrance was by a delightful children's playground, with large statues of dinosaurs in it. Inside the palace was a hall of mirrors, not unlike the building in Shiraz, and many of the walls were covered with murals showing scenes from Safavid history; this was where the rulers used to receive foreign envoys.

Cehel Sotun Palace, Isfahan.

We also met a group of younger schoolchildren there, but their teachers did not allow them to pester us, though we were not discouraged from taking a photograph of the party.

After this, we were driven to what is normally considered the most beautiful part of Isfahan, the Maydan Imam Square. This square was three times the size of St Mark's Square in Venice: 500 metres long and 160 metres wide. The mosques were all covered both inside and out with blue tiles. We went first to the Ali Qapu, or as it is often called, Safavid Palace. We climbed the steep steps to the first floor, where there was a magnificent view of the whole place. Indeed, it was from here that the early rulers used to view their military parades and the polo matches which used to take place below. It was also possible to see clearly that the fine Masjid-I Imam Mosque at the east end of Maydan Imam Square, completed in 1638, was set at an angle of forty-five degrees to the square so that it had the correct direction towards Mecca, whereas the square itself had an exact west-east orientation. Up another steep set of stairs was the music room, where the king and his guest were entertained by musicians. Niches in the shape of bowls and high-stemmed flasks were dug into the wall, which reportedly made for fine acoustics as well as for decoration.

Safavid Palace in the Maydan Imam Square, Isfahan.

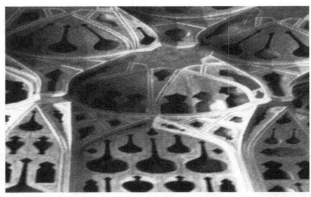

Music room in the palace.

Immediately opposite the Ali Qapu stood the Sheik Lotfollah Mosque, which was probably used by the women of the royal harem. It had a fine dome and was also decorated with blue tiles, but it did not have the correct orientation towards Mecca.

Maydan Imam Square, Isfahan.

However, the finest of the buildings in the square was undoubtedly the mosque known as Masjid-I Imam, situated at the east end; with its two tall minarets at the entrance portal and another two by the entrance to the mosque itself, it dominated the whole area. The semi dome at the rear of the towering entrance was under scaffolding and was being retiled, I imagine with the same blue tiling of the main dome. The courtyard walls were all also covered with decorated tiling which was, to my mind, right up to the standard of the work I had seen the previous year in Samarkand. The inside of the mosque was equally highly decorated, and the inside of the dome was unbelievable.

Maydan Imam Square, Isfahan.

Masjid-I Imam Mosque, Isfahan.

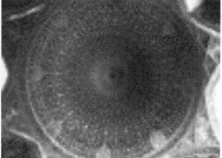

Masjid-I Imam Mosque, Isfahan.

The square itself was surrounded by a low corridor, with shops on either side forming a bazaar, though the bazaar area on the western side was as large as the rest put together, with a number of further covered streets and shops branching off away from the open area. One of these streets was devoted to metal makers, who were hard at work, though otherwise there was no one area devoted to any one trade. The first time I entered the bazaar, most of the shops were closed. The government had suddenly removed subsidies from various commodities, including some foods, and many of the shops had shut for one day in a form of protest. However, my next visit was much more interesting, as trade was buzzing.

We were taken as a group to a shop where carpets and rugs were made and sold. We walked down some steps into a basement area, and at the bottom of the steps, I found myself walking on an unmistakeable Balucci rug like the one I had at home. The proprietor was startled that an elderly British citizen like me should recognise this. I had not meant to buy anything here but fell for a Persian rug; after much haggling (a process I normally hate), I bought it for half the original asking price as a present for Elinor.

Though the Maydan Imam Square was the largest attraction in Isfahan, it was by no means the only one. We were also taken to see the Armenian Cathedral. There was a large community of Armenians in Isfahan, and when we visited, the church was crowded. The population of Armenians in the area was now thought to be about seven thousand, a very large decrease from 1960, when it was estimated at one hundred thousand. However, there were still some thirteen churches in the area. The cathedral had been rebuilt in the mid-seventeenth century, with a separate bell tower added in 1764. The outside was attractive but nothing special; however, the interior wall paintings and tile work, all dating from

1660 to 1670, were remarkable. Unluckily, interior photography was not allowed. An official inside told me that freedom of worship here was not discouraged in any way. A building in the precincts had a display of photographs and other artefacts dealing with the genocide in Turkey. There was a display in the courtyard of pictures by schoolchildren marking the anniversary of the start of the genocide on 24 April 1915, demanding an apology from the Turks. Jacynth and I had seen a similar exhibition in Armenia many years before. If only the Turks would just make an apology, nothing more would be needed. I think it might make a very great difference to politics in the area, for it is just pride that stops them doing so at the moment.

Armenian cathedral, Isfahan.   *Bell tower of Armenian cathedral.*

The area near the cathedral was also attractive to look at, mainly nineteenth century, with many small cafés and shops among the houses. Quite a number of the shop advertisements were in English, several of which amused me. One read "Handing Crafts"; another, "Fake Jewellery" in very large letters outside a jewellers; and "Milk Sheiks" in a shop that sold ice cream.

We were also taken to see some of the bridges over the Zayandeh River. The river bed itself was almost empty when we saw it, for the authorities had dammed the river above the city, which they do occasionally, in order to clear it of weeds; we saw huge piles of these being carried away by fleets of lorries. Although this meant that we could not see the views at their best, we were able to walk under the bridges and see their full length from below and also see where the water level normally came up to. We saw the Khaju Bridge, built in the fifteenth century, which had twenty-two arches and a central kiosk two storeys high. We walked across the bridge to the gardens on the other side, where there was a small brick shrine to Hafez, the great Iranian poet. While we were there, a group of girls from a local university were the busy sketching the shrine. We then went on to see the Allahverdi Khan Bridge, built in 1603, with its thirty-three arches.

Khaju Bridge, Isfahan.

Allahverdi Khan Bridge, Isfahan.

Another building we saw was the vast Masjid-I Mosque, parts of which date back to the tenth century; it was steadily expanded over the years, finally enclosing a large courtyard with buildings in many different styles. The earliest part is brick alone, but much of the later work has considerable tile decoration.

Masjid-I Mosque, Isfahan.

Masjid-I Mosque, Isfahan.

Masjid-I Mosque, Isfahan.

Our next journey was back to Tehran via Kashan. The first stop was to inspect a qanat. Qanats are underground water channels, some of them hundreds of years old, bringing the much-needed water from the mountains to the towns and fields in the more desert regions. Most of them have been superseded by proper piped water mains, but we were told that the one we visited was still in operation and fed a village we could see in the distance.

Kashan was an interesting town We stopped by the remains of the defensive walls. From here, we could see the conical shape of one of the large ice houses which were so necessary before the days of electric freezers. There were also in the town a large number of *badgers*, or wind towers. These towers are designed to trap the wind and pull it down, cooling it on the way to keep cool a house, water tank, or ice house. They are a remarkably efficient form of air conditioning, without the need of electricity, and much needed in some of the desert habitations, where temperatures can reach 50 degrees Celsius in the summer months. I stood by one in an hotel and was startled by how cool the air was coming from it. Some of these towers were elaborately decorated by owners trying to show off their importance. One we saw even resembled a mosque.

City walls, Kashan.   *Wind towers, Kashan.*

While in Kashan, we were taken to see the original home of a prominent tea merchant that was now a museum. It had a large wooden double entry door, and each half had a knocker on it. Our guide demonstrated on each of these knockers to show that they made different sounds; women used one, and men the other so that the sex of the person wanting to enter would be known before the door was opened.

The building itself was most interesting, with a large, sunken inner courtyard containing a rectangular pool. All the rooms of the house were entered from this courtyard. The building itself was, of course, kept cool with the aid of the wind towers, including the one designed to look like a mosque. The walls and the rooms were decorated with carvings and murals. There were several houses like this one, which gives you a good idea of the luxury in which the rich lived.

Nearby was a public baths complex that was no longer operative. This was also highly decorated, and from its roof, there was an excellent view of the town and all its wind towers. Both the house and the bath house had quite a number of visitors, since it was a weekend, and many people had come out for the day from Tehran, though the majority of them had also come to see the famous Bagh-I Fin gardens, which we visited next.

Merchant's house, Kashan.

Public baths, Kashan.

We spent some time in the gardens themselves and also made use of the open air café, well shaded under trees. This garden was built by the Safavid dynasty. Although it has been much repaired and restored over the years, it still kept most of its original layout, including a central pavilion placed over water channels, where people could dip their hands, possibly as some form of worship. There were certainly religiously minded men there, for when the call to prayer came over the muezzin, they laid out their rugs by one of the water channels, knelt down, and said their prayers looking towards Mecca. Like all of the many gardens we saw during our visit to Iran, water played a large part in the lay-out.

Bagh-I Fin Gardens, Kashan.

Café in the Bagh-I Fin Gardens, Kashan.

An unexpected event was to make our return to Tehran particularly memorable. Our small coach broke down, luckily only a hundred yards from the entrance to a motorway service station. We made our way there on foot, expecting a long wait, but our guide met a coach driver he knew who was returning to Tehran after a day's outing and who had room to fit us all in. The middle-aged and elderly travellers in the coach were quite happy to take us on board. They were highly respectable-looking women and men. As soon as the coach left the service station, its curtains were drawn so no one could see in, music started blaring forth, and several of the women stood up and started dancing in the aisle. They ripped their hijabs off their heads and waved them in the air, with those who were still seated laughing and clapping. Needless to say, we were told not to take photographs, since uncovering your head in public is illegal for women in Iran. By the time we arrived back in Tehran, they were all sitting demurely in their seats with their heads once again covered. This shows that it was not only young travellers who did not like the strict religious laws.

That evening, we had a farewell dinner together, since this was the end of the tour. However, I had booked an extension to go and see the city of Yazd. For this, I was to have my own personal guide who came with me for the internal flight to Yazd Airport, where we were picked up by our driver in a very comfortable car. My guide and I were to stay for two nights in the Moshir Garden Hotel, which was another traditional house hotel, set in yet another delightful garden. When we arrived, we were greeted by two brightly coloured parakeets, one of whom used to be transferred to a perch in the dining room during the evening meal. The staff had been taken by surprise a few days before when one of them had laid an egg, for they had both been thought to be male (they still do not know which is which).

Moshir Garden Hotel, Yazd.

After a rest and some lunch, for we had started at an early hour to catch the plane, our driver appeared again and took us on a tour of the city. Yazd was set in the desert but not far from the mountains, over which we had flown from Tehran. It had an old centre and several fine mosques and wind towers but also many high-rise modern buildings. On the way into the old town, for our hotel was some way from the centre, we stopped by the bazaar so I could buy a new sunhat (for I had left my old one in the taxi on the way to the airport in Tehran; incidentally, it was waiting for me when we returned to Tehran). We then visited the Masdid-I Jami, a lovely mosque with two tall minarets covered with soft green tiles. There was a rectangular pond in front of this with small fountains and, at the further end, the statues of three water workers; water is very important to towns in the desert, though we never saw signs of any shortages, and we were told that now the supply being brought from the nearby mountains was excellent (some of the more remote settlements in the desert had to be careful though). Outside this mosque stood a most peculiar structure called a *nakhal*, which is made of date palm and looks like a woven trellis, almost heart shaped at each end with a point at the top. This was used for carrying coffins; some of them were so large that they need fifty people to carry them.

Masdid-I Jami mosque, Yazd.   *Coffin carrier in front of Masdid-I Jami mosque.*

Quite a lot of the old town was built of mud bricks baked in the sun; one of these buildings was an old caravanserai, which was now gradually disintegrating. We also saw the new Zoroastrian temple with a pool in front.

Zoroastrian temple, Yazd. My guide and I with Zoroastrians.

The Zoroastrian, or fire worshiping, religion is possibly the oldest religion now extant. There are still supposed to be over ten thousand Zoroastrians living in the villages around Yazd. The modern temple held the sacred fire which is never extinguished; it had to be carried, still alight, from its previous home when the temple was built. We were then driven to a Zoroastrian village, where we were invited in to have tea and biscuits by an old lady who was responsible for the care of the sacred tree, supposedly over a thousand years old. Our next stop was by one of several "Towers of Silence" in the area. These "towers" were circular walls at the top of a hill. Near the bottom of each hill were the ruins of a settlement where the bodies of the dead fire worshippers were taken. The priest had then to carry the body up to the tower and deposit it inside the walls. No one else was allowed there. The body was then left for the vultures to come and pick clean. When this had finally happened, the priest would go up again and bring the cleaned bones down, and they would be buried in an urn. This macabre practice was now illegal; the dead were buried in concrete in burial areas so that the rotting flesh cannot contaminate the earth. We were told that this was the only way in which the authorities had interfered with this religion. The next afternoon, we visited another site where there were two of these towers; I am glad to say that I was able to scale the hill right up to both of them.

Old Zoroastrian settlement and Tower of Silence, Yazd.

The next day, we drove about fifty kilometres out into the desert to a town called Meybod. This was a particularly interesting little town, for it had few new buildings in it, and almost every structure was made with mud bricks baked in the sun, so it had a very desert-type colour, for it was, in fact, from the desert sand that the bricks were made. We drove first to the ruined citadel, from whose walls we were able to see the whole town and in whose courtyard new bricks were being made for repairs. Nearby was an old caravanserai, one of the rooms of which was being used for people to make carpets and other textiles. There was also a very large ice house with no fewer than four wind towers to keep the ice from melting. There was another school party of young boys waiting to enter, and when my guide returned with the key, their teachers persuaded him to instruct them all about it, since no official was available. It was interesting that some thirty of us filled much less than a quarter of the way round the path on which we were standing, and the depth below was considerable. It was very chilly in the ice house, though it was hot outside.

Mud brick citadel, Meybod.

Brick making, Meybod. Ice house, Meybod.

Our final visit in Meybod was to a pigeon tower on the outskirts of the town. These edifices were supposed to hold many thousands of pigeons each. They had no windows, and the white stripe around the tower was designed to stop snakes climbing up and getting in. The solitary door was opened only once a year so people could enter to collect the guano.

Pigeon tower, Meybod.

When we returned by air to Tehran, we found our taxi waiting for us, with my sun hat. During the journey back to the hotel, my guide, who had been talking to the driver, suddenly burst into a roar of laughter. He then turned to me and said, "He wants to know if you do martial arts." I said no and asked why he thought I might.

"Well, I told him that you had climbed to the top of the Towers of Silence, which he knows, and he thought you must keep very fit to be able to do that and wondered if you did martial arts to keep fit." It was obviously meant as a great compliment to me.

So ended my tour to Iran, a tour which proved even more interesting than I had expected, not so much for the architecture, which was marvellous, as were the classical sites, but also for the gardens and even more the people, who were far more friendly and open than I had ever expected. I am so glad to have gone when I did, for the political situation has worsened so much recently. I do not think it would be possible to do the trip now. Once again, I gained the impression that if only it were left to ordinary people and not to politicians, the world would be a far better and safer place.

Carpet weaving, Yazd.

Mosque, Yazd.

Statues of water sellers, Yazd.

Friday Mosque, Shiraz.

CHAPTER 8

SOUTHEAST TURKEY: THE CRADLE OF CIVILISATION

Mount Ararat, Turkey.

My next trip in 2011 was to be to the southeast corner of Turkey. I flew to Adana via Istanbul, where I met my driver. I had been told it would be Murat, from the previous year, but he was unable to come, so I was met by Sinan, who was to drive me for the whole of my visit. Luckily, he spoke excellent English and proved to be every bit as skilful a driver as Murat. This time, I had merely said where I wished to visit and left the actual itinerary to Anatolian Sky, since I knew the roads had improved and the hotels had changed since my last visit.

The Inci Hotel in Adana proved to be one that Jacynth and I had stayed in before. It was a very pleasant hotel and much preferable to the larger pretentious hotel nearby, in which we had also stayed.

The next day, we drove to Antakya, the ancient Antioch on the Orontes, in the Hatay area. The road down past the seaside town of Iskenderun and up over the Belen pass had improved greatly, so that we arrived before noon, instead of taking a full day, as had been the case in my earlier visits. We went first to our hotel, which proved to be in Harbiye, a few miles to the south. Sinan went off to find a bed for himself (he never stayed in the same hotel as me, probably due to the cost), and I went to have lunch in an open air café nearby. While I was lunching, a group sat down at the table behind me, and I suddenly heard someone speaking English. He said, "This food is much better than I had ever expected." The group proved to be journalists from the *Sunday Telegraph* who had just come out to interview refugees from Syria who had fled from the troubles which had recently started there. They proved to be the only English travellers I met on this trip. When we were leaving the next morning, a Turkish television crew arrived on the same quest.

After lunch, we started with a visit to the Cave Church of St Peter and St Paul above Antioch. This was where St Peter and his followers were first called Christians; it claims to be the earliest church in the world.

Cave Church of St Peter and St Paul, Antioch on the Orontes.

I was normally sceptical about attributions of early events to certain places, but this one, I think, may be the truth. It was the only cave that I have seen near Antioch that would be suitable; there was even a tunnel, now collapsed, which could have been used for escape in case of emergency. The stone front was built by the Crusaders, so the tradition dates back a long time. It was still used for the occasional services, including the appropriate saints' days. There had obviously been an increase in visiting, for on my previous visits, there had seldom been anyone else there, but now the path up to it was lined with stalls selling tourist tat. It was noticeable, however, that not many of the visitors passed through the entrance gate, where a charge was being levied.

My main reason for wishing to go to Antioch was to see the museum; while it had a few fine sarcophagi and Hittite statues, it was mainly famous for its wonderful collection of Roman mosaics. It was sometimes called the finest collection of its type in the world. I do not think it is as fine as the Bardo in Tunis, but it is certainly among the best. The finds at Zeugma may be even finer, but there were only a few of them, and the collections in Tripoli in Libya and El Djem in Tunisia, while excellent, were no better.

Museum in Antioch on the Orontes.

There were literally hundreds of mosaics; some of the largest were on the floor, but most of them hung on the walls. There were even a few in an open (but roofed) walkway outside. I had allowed a long time for the visit, but when I emerged, I still had time to walk around the old part of Antioch. It was one of the few places in Turkey that church bells can be heard ringing. I even had time to visit the attractive Orthodox church before meeting Sinan and returning to the hotel in Harbiye.

Harbiye was the place where most of the mosaics had been discovered, and opposite my hotel, I found a rough track that led down a steep slope to some waterfalls, where the ancient settlement had been. There were now several open air restaurants among the woods, one of which was actually named Mosaics, though there were now no traces of the remains left.

Orthodox church, Antioch.   *Mosaics Restaurant, with waterfalls, Harbiye.*

The next day, we set off to Gaziantep to see the brand-new Zeugma Museum, in which were displayed the magnificent mosaics rescued from Zeugma (which was now flooded by a new reservoir). Jacynth and I had actually visited Zeugma while the waters were rising and some frantic last-minute rescue work was being done. On a later visit, we had seen some of the rescued mosaics on display in the Gaziantep Archaeological Museum, and after mentioning the name of Louis Schofield (who had been in charge of the final rescue work and whom we had met back in England), we had seen some of the other mosaics being restored.

On the way, we turned off the main road and went to visit Yesemek, where a museum had been established on the site of the old Hittite quarries, where most of the stone for the statues had been dug out and carved. Jacynth and I had visited this place twice before and never met any other visitors. It was to be the same again, except that the place had been much tidied up, and there was now a small shop. The curator took me round the whole site and would not accept a tip at the end, though I did buy several fridge magnets in the shop, carved to look like some of the unfinished sculptures still lying around.

Open air Hittite Quarry Museum, Yesemek.

After a very enjoyable visit and a refreshing drink in the shop, we drove on to Gaziantep and followed the many signposts to the new gallery. Here, we were to be disappointed, for despite its official opening date having been six weeks earlier, only the shop was open, and we were told that its opening would now not be for another six weeks. The officials had not even informed their own citizens of the change, for while we were there, a coach with schoolchildren arrived. We gathered they had taken the precaution of booking in advance, so my hopes were raised, as I hatched a plan to be admitted with them as some sort of foreign language teacher. Unfortunately, they too were turned away.

We now decided to go and see a castle which was down on our itinerary as at Gaziantep, even though it proved to be in a town forty kilometres away. When we arrived at that town, we found the castle was another forty kilometres farther on. Still, we decided to make for it, until we almost at once ran into road works and found, on asking, that these went on for almost the whole distance. Knowing the awfulness of most Turkish road works, Sinan and I unanimously decided to give up; we stopped for lunch before returning to Gaziantep, where we found my hotel, an extraordinary seventeen-storey building a few miles out of town. I had an excellent evening meal in the restaurant on the top floor, with a marvellous all-round view. I was surprised to find there were only two other people in the huge room.

The next day, we travelled on to Sanliurfa and, after some difficulty, found my delightful, and much smaller, hotel, with a lovely view of the citadel from my room.

Hotel in Gaziantep. *View of citadel from Urfa Hotel.*

I spent the rest of the afternoon walking around Urfa: the citadel, the sacred pool of Abraham, and the delightful bazaar. Early in the first millennium, it was called Edessa, the Holy City. According to Turkish legend, Abraham was born there, in a cave at the bottom of the cliff, and not in Ur, as is commonly believed. There was now a large mosque in front of this cave, on the site of an old Christian church, and a large number of pilgrims queued up to visit the cave. I did not join them, since I had gone in there before. Later, also according to legend, Abraham angered the king, who ordered him to be killed by being thrown over the cliff into a large fire below. However, as he fell, the fire was turned into water, and Abraham was saved by landing in the water. The place was now a sacred pool filled by sacred fish, which must not be harmed in any way. Edessa was also where the Holy Cloth (which was supposedly placed over the face of the dead Jesus and imprinted with an image of his face) was kept for centuries. It disappeared during the Crusades, but some people believe that it was taken back to Europe and is now known as the Holy Shroud of Turin. The whole area, including sacred Islamic buildings, was set in a delightful park.

I also climbed up the very steep path to the ruins of the citadel and two ancient columns, from where there was a magnificent view over the city. It was possible to see an old Roman basilica which was now put to good use as an electricity sub-station (one of the most remarkable pieces of recycling that I have ever encountered). The bazaar, most of which was covered, was very near to this area; it was a typical Middle Eastern market area. I enjoyed walking around the area, though Sinan complained that he could not find anyone who spoke Turkish; they all spoke just Kurdish, which he could not understand.

Abraham's Pool, Urfa.

Urfa by night.

Abraham's Pool, Urfa.

The next day, we drove over the flat plain to visit Harran. The first time I had seen this area, it had been mainly desert, but now with new reservoirs and the damming of the Euphrates, plenty of water was able to be piped, and the whole area was growing fruit and crops.

Harran was where, according to the Bible, Abraham had gone to live; I had expected it to be a hive of tourists. When we had to pay to drive the car through the entrance gate and saw several stalls selling memorabilia, I thought my fears were going to be realised. But while we were visiting, only one other car was there, and it left just after we arrived, and there was one small coach with Turkish visitors. Harran was famous for its beehive-shaped houses, and I was pleased to see many of these were still being lived in. One house was now a sort of house museum, which we were able to visit to see how people lived there.

Harran.   *Harran.*

At the start of my walk around, I was pressed by an official guide to take him, for he said I was certain to be pestered by other non-official guides and children. In the event, only one other person asked me politely if he could help me in any way. I was interested to see again the tall square minaret, which Lawrence of Arabia had mistakenly thought was the tower of a long lost cathedral.

Back at the hotel in Urfa, I met a couple of pleasant American ladies, who asked me if I had been to Gobekli Tepe. I admitted I had never even heard of it. They told me I really must visit it, since it was only some twelve kilometres distant from Urfa. They also said that the latest edition of *National Geographic* magazine had it as its main article. So when we left the next morning, we followed their advice, and I was so glad we did. It was an archaeological site carbon dated to between 9,500 and 7,500 BC, far and away the world's oldest discovered temple. To date, they had only excavated about 10 percent of the site and discovered three circular chambers, the standing stones of which had been completely smoothed, unlike Stonehenge, with animals and insects carved on them. How hunter-gatherers were capable of constructing such a monument was not yet known. When we visited, there was no one else there except for the resident guard, photographer, and archaeologist, who kindly showed me around. Luckily, for he spoke not a word of English, several exhibits had boards explaining matters in both Turkish and English. It was one of the most exciting places I had ever seen and more than made up for the disappointment about Zeugma.

Gobekli Tepe Temple, near Urfa.

I spent quite a time at Gobekli Tepe, ending up with drinking a cup of tea with Sinan and the resident guard, who showed us a number of photographs of the excavations in action as well as a much-thumbed copy of *National Geographic,* which had only been published a couple of weeks before. He was obviously proud of it, though he could only rely on the photographs because of his lack of English; I imagined he showed it to all of his infrequent foreign visitors.

We then set off for the town of Malatya, stopping on the way for lunch near Kahta. Sinan said he could not understand why we were not staying there for the night, since it was the usual stopping-off place for a visit to Mount Nemrut Dag, and that we would have to drive back the seventy or so kilometres over the mountain to Kahta to get there. I said I had been told there was another way to Nemrut direct from Malatya, where we would have to stay in any case if we were to see the extraordinary mosque at Divrigi; the agents had probably decided three nights in one hotel was the best option. The road from Kahta to Malatya took us over some lovely mountains and was in good condition (except where road works promised that eventually the whole seventy or so kilometres would be easy driving). Malatya itself was a pleasant town where Jacynth and I had stayed twice before. The hotel proved to be very comfortable and was in a good position from where I was able to explore. It was a town where the different trades tended to stick together; I even saw a water seller offering his wares from a water container on his back. Many erstwhile water sellers now sell water from the taps, and bottled water has become easily available, but this man was still selling real water and seemed to get plenty of custom.

Water seller, Malatya.

Cobbler, Malatya.

Malatya mosque.

The next morning, the weather had changed for the worse; there was drizzle in the air and the skies were threatening worse to come. Ever since the day we left Antioch, the forecast had been promising rain, and we gathered there had been very bad storms back in Adana. Now the bad weather seemed to have caught up with us. We had intended to go to Mount Nemrut Dag, but it did not seem a good thing to go up a mountain with most of the sightseeing on foot and in the open air, so we decided to use this day to travel to Divrigi instead and hoped for the best. It rained steadily for our long drive up the main road, but when we turned off for the forty or so kilometres to Divrigi, the rain became more intermittent, and we even saw a few patches of blue in the sky. There was damp in the air and some drizzle for the whole of our visit, but no heavy rain.

The purpose of our visit was to see the old mosque with the attached sanatorium, which was dedicated in 1228. Very few tourists come here, for it is far from the beaten track, and it is a long way to go to see a single building. Jacynth and I had been once before, and I especially wanted to come again, for on our previous visit, it had been closed for restoration inside, and I wanted to see that as well as the most extraordinary exterior. There were four doorways to the building, three on the long front and one at one end. Each of these entrances was decorated with the most remarkable intricate carvings of fauna, flora, and pure decoration. There was certainly no other building like it in Turkey. Inside, the mihrab was plain but the ceiling and the many supporting columns were highly (though not as extravagantly) decorated. I was disappointed to see that the floor was now covered with a single patterned carpet instead of the many multi-coloured rugs which would have been there originally. Many old mosque rugs can now be found in Turkish museums, though a few mosques, especially ones with wooden columns, in the north and east of the country, have not yet been modernised in this manner.

The Divrigi Mosque.

We stopped for lunch at a little café in a settlement at the junction with the main road. One, of many, good things to be said for Turkey is that even the most unappealing-looking sort of place usually serves good (and sometimes excellent) food. While we were driving back, Sinan told me that he had called in to the police station the previous evening to enquire about the road to Nemrut. They had advised him very strongly to go via Kahta, since while it was much farther in distance, the quality of the direct road from Malatya was terrible and it was much easier, and probably would be quicker, to go back through Kahta. From that point of view, it would probably have been better to spend one night in Kahta, see Nemrut, and then travel on to stay just two nights in Malatya, but we had been lucky, in view of the weather, to have done it the way we did.

The next day, the weather was much better, and though showers threatened once or twice, most of the time it was sunny and warm. We drove the long way back to Kahta, where we took the road towards the famous mountain. There was now a fine road for the greater part of the way, but we turned off onto the old road in order to see some of the lower sites. King Antiochus of the small kingdom of Commagene, a client king of Rome, had visions of grandeur and decided to build himself a temple complex at the top of the tallest mountain in his kingdom; when he died, he was buried under what is believed to be the world's largest man-made mound. This mound, on top of the mountain, was made entirely of small stones; it was between fifty and sixty metres high and covered an area of over seven acres. Antiochus, however, did not consider his wife merited the same importance, so he had her tomb, known as the Karakus, built with a smaller (but nevertheless quite large) mound; it was on a smaller hill at a considerable distance, but still visible, from Nemrut Dag. The old road was much windier and narrower but now completely free of traffic.

The mound had three separate columns on different sides, which were originally surmounted by carvings of animals or birds (the name *Karakus* means "blackbird"). The first column one saw on approaching the tumulus was the best preserved, with an eagle on top of it, and there was a lion's head standing by itself on the ground, in a good state of preservation. There was also a fine view, across the river valley, to Nemrut Dag itself, with its tumulus clearly visible despite the distance. The road then dropped down to the Roman bridge across the river.

Karakus column near Nemrui.

View to Nemrut from Karakus.

Lion's head, Karakus.

The Roman bridge, built by Emperor Septimius Severus about the year AD 210, originally had two columns at each end. However, when his eldest son, Caracalla, became joint emperor with his younger brother, Geta, he had Geta murdered so that he could rule alone. Caracalla pulled down the column dedicated to Geta in an effort to erase all memory of his name. The first time Jacynth and I came to the area, we drove across this bridge, but motorised access to it was now blocked and a new bridge built nearby, all this despite the fact there was so little traffic. A fine new restaurant which had been built on the hillside above was now deserted, and all that was left was one run-down shop.

Some way on was Commagene, the ancient summer capital of Arsameia. Here we encountered a middle-aged Dutch couple. We had been told at the ticket office at Caracus that this pair had been there and were the only visitors before us. I met them again at the top of Nemrut Dag but met no other visitors all day. Here, in Arsameia, there was a truncated relief stele of the god Mithras, a man-made cave with a tunnel, which I did not descend, running down to what is believed to be a Mithraic cult chamber. Up a rough path, there was a statue of Hercules and Antiochus shaking hands. There was not much to see here, but what there was, was impressive, and it was well worth the drive on the old road.

Statues at Arsameia, near Mount Nemrut.

We then drove on and kept to the old road until we hit the new and followed that before turning off onto the road that led to Mount Nemrut itself. The improvement in the road surface since I had last visited was tremendous, and that had been a great improvement over earlier visits. The ticket office and other buildings had also improved since my last visit and now even included a few beds for the night, though apparently one had to provide one's own bedding There were now two paths up to the top; I chose the one to the East Terrace, since that was the higher and from then on, it would be all downhill. It was quite a climb up the rough track; I later read in a guide book that the terrace was six hundred metres higher than the car park. Once again, I found the climb well worth it. The East Terrace had a line of gigantic seated figures in front of the tumulus. All their heads were detached and lined up in front of them. The heads themselves were as tall as a human figure.

The East Terrace of Mount Nemrut, with the tumulus behind.

The statues were guarded on each side by a lion and an eagle. They consisted of Antiochus himself with several deities, and there was still the base of what used to be a temple in front, which was now marked with a large letter H, evidently for a helicopter pad, should it be necessary. There were also a lot of clearly visible inscriptions carved on the backs of the row of seated statues. The first time I was here was for the sunrise, and the effect was magical, as the statues gradually appeared out of the darkness into the light. The disadvantage was that it was bitterly cold, even in mid-summer, and there were crowds of young people, who had come up in numerous minibuses to see the sight. At this time of day, there was no one at all there except for me and, later, the Dutch couple, so there was plenty of time to wander round inspecting.

I next descended a little to the North Terrace which, although levelled, had no statues. It was thought that it was probably used as an assembly place. The West Terrace (there was no South Terrace) was a little lower than the North and also consisted of a large number of statues and low reliefs. Some of the reliefs had been removed to a huge shed below the North Terrace for repair, so I could not see them, including, sadly, the Zodiac lion, which was one of my favourites; however, the rest were there, and for me this terrace gave the best view.

The West Terrace, Mount Nemrut.

Statues on the West Terrace, Mount Nemrut.

I returned to the car park by the other path and was very glad I had chosen the route I had, for there were some very awkward areas on this path which were easier going down than they would have been going up. We stopped at a small open air roadside café for a welcomed cup of tea on our way back to Malatya.

The next day, we travelled to Batman with a stop at Diyarbakir, which was one of the most religious towns in Turkey and had the oldest mosque (as well as some of the finest city walls, though rather grim since they were built of black basalt). They surpassed even those of Avila in Spain. Not long after leaving Malatya, we passed a sign pointing towards Nemrut Dag, and at that point, the road did not look bad. If one did approach Nemrut from this direction, the climb from the car park to the top was considerably less, but I am not sure how one can manage to see the Karakus and Roman bridge and Arsemeia.

I had a slight disappointment in Diyarbakir, since the Ulu Jami (Old Mosque) proved to be closed for restoration; even its courtyard was mainly blocked off. However, I was able to see one of the fine outbuildings with its exterior carvings. I also visited the bazaar and had quite a long walk by the city walls.

The Old Mosque, Diyarbakir. *Part of city walls, Diyarbakir.*

It was not a long drive from Diyarbakir to Batman, and along the roadside, most of the telegraph poles had a stork's nest on top. I had forgotten this remarkable sight in this area. When we arrived in Batman, we drove straight to the so-called four-star Asko Hotel. From outside, it looked fine, but inside proved to be possibly the worst hotel I had ever stayed in anywhere. Here is a list, in no particular order, of my reasons for this statement:

1. There were water stains on the ceiling of my bedroom.
2. The carpets throughout the hotel were very dirty and badly stained.
3. The badly painted cream walls were often black with dirt when they reached the ceiling.
4. The curtain in my bedroom was torn.
5. I had a torn and stained chair cover in my bedroom.

6. My very coarse bathroom towel had frayed edges.
7. There were holes in the wall filled with grey unrepainted plaster.
8. The plaster in the bathroom between the door frame and the wall was cracked and falling out in places.
9. The cover of the electric wiring to the air conditioning was cracked and not fitting into the wall correctly.
10. There was cheap wooden furniture, badly fitting, with one knob missing and its screw point sticking out into the room.
11. The balcony door frame was dusty, and the lock did not function.
12. The dressing table was very dusty, and the light above it was disintegrating.
13. New (?) cheap handles to the bathroom door did not fit where the old handles were, and the gaps were left unpainted.
14. The tops of the wall floor skirtings were filthy.
15. Some of the water pipes in the bathroom looked as if they had not been cleaned for years, and there was spattered paint on the screw handles to turn the water supply to the room off.
16. In the breakfast bar, the paint was peeling off the ceiling.
17. The breakfast was far and away the worst of any hotel I had stayed in during many visits to Turkey. There was not even any coffee.
18. Neither the restaurant nor bar was ever open, and both looked as if they were permanently shut.
19. There were not even any pictures on the walls.
20. The bath was very old and worn.

I did think of asking to change to another room, but a quick look in several showed them to be in the same state. The only thing to be said on the plus side was that the sheets, towel, and basin were fairly clean, and the room was of a reasonably four-star size. Needless to say, I ate out for my two evenings there and was lucky to find a very pleasant open air restaurant which served good food. I would advise anyone who wishes to stay in the area to do so at Diyarbakir, where such hotels as the Dedeman and others of a smaller size are very satisfactory, and it is possible to reach the same places on a day trip.

The first place we went to visit was Hasankeyf, now threatened with being destroyed by the Ilisu Dam, which is due to be built shortly on the River Tigris. There was much opposition to this, as the cliff city is a world heritage site and the original plan for the dam was dropped when several international firms withdrew their funding, but the plan has recently been put in play once more. Driving from Batman, we reached the Tigris River and drove along the bank till we came to the Zeyn El-Abin Turbesi, a construction of a style unique in Turkey. It was under scaffolding for restoration, but whether this will be carried out in view of the dam project is doubtful, for it would be covered by the water.

Zeyn El-Abin Turbesi.

Distant view of Hasankeyf.

I was lucky while I was here, for a man appeared with a key who ushered me inside so that I was able to see the brickwork of the underside of the dome and the few remaining blue wall tiles. From outside, there was a view to the cliff city, so we drove on until we reached the bridge over the river, where we stopped and I took photographs of the remaining piers of the old Roman bridge. Sinan had a conversation with a motorcyclist who had also stopped there, because motorcycles are a passion for him. We then drove on through a very narrow street to a café near the entrance of the old cave city. For some reason, I was waved through without having to pay for my ticket and was able to climb up the steep path to the top.

Remains of Roman bridge, Hasankeyf.

Hasankeyf minaret.

Another Hasankeyf minaret.

View of Hasankeyf from upper cave city.

A rather amusing incident occurred while I was up at the top. A group of six Germans appeared, and I started talking with one of them, who spoke good English. I asked him if they were having a good trip, and he said they would be were it not for one of their party; he pointed to one man who, he said, kept on boasting that he must have been the oldest man ever to have climbed up to that point. I asked how old he was; he was seventy-seven. I then acted rather disgracefully and asked if the person concerned spoke English and was told that the whole party did. So a little later on, I started talking with him, and sure enough, he started boasting to me that he must be the oldest person ever to have climbed up to this point.

"Oh," I asked, "how old are you?" Then when he told me I said, "You are still a young man. I am eighty-two."

The rest of the group who were listening all burst into a roar of laughter He looked shattered but then tried to recover.

"However," he said, "I did climb up Nemrut Dag a few days ago."

"Oh," I replied, "I was up there the day before yesterday. I've got some photos here on my camera."

It was disgraceful of me, I know, but it made the day, and possibly the rest of their holiday, for the others in that group.

There was plenty to see up at the top, including the remains of old mosques, churches, and cave houses, even though part of it was closed because of the danger of rock falls.

After leaving Hasankeyf, we drove on to the town of Midyat, where we stopped for lunch. Midyat was interesting, having a Christian quarter with several churches. We went to this area on our return from the monastery of Mar Gabriel, the oldest surviving Syrian Orthodox monastery in Turkey, which almost closed during the Kurdish troubles, but under the guidance of the magnificent bishop, whom I met on my previous visit, it had increased the size of its community from about fifteen to sixty at the time of this visit. He had also arranged for the Christian children in Midyat to come on Fridays, the Muslim holy day, to be instructed about the Christian religion and to learn Aramaic, which was still used in its services. Under his rule, many new buildings had been erected, usually by Muslim craftsmen.

Monastery of Mar Gabriel, near Midyat.

On our return to Midyat, we drove to the Christian quarter, hoping to see one of the churches there. Unfortunately, both of the churches we looked at were shut and locked. However, we then spotted what looked like a monastery at a little distance, and when we reached it, we found a mainly new building, possibly on the site of an earlier place of worship. There were quite a number of visitors, all Turkish and many of them Muslims, who treated this Christian place with great respect. The buildings seemed to be built in the same style as those at Mar Gabriel, some of them still not yet finished. Inside the church part of the building, I was impressed by a fine modern tomb. Outside the gate, there was a newly made open air café, under some trees, with little statues of animals and people of a sort to amuse children. It seemed clear that in this part of the country, the Muslims and Christians lived together in a welcome harmony. Long may it last.

Monastery in Midyat.   *Tomb in Midyat Monastery.*

Our next day's journey was to take us to Van, by the lake of that name, where I was to spend the last four nights of my holiday. Lake Van itself was at an altitude of 1,750 metres and had an area of approximately 4,000 square kilometres. It was not so long ago that the best way to travel from one end of the lake to the other was to take a ferry; indeed, a friend of mine just did that, but the improvement of the roads had made that unnecessary. We started along the northern side of the lake, because I wanted to see the great Armenian and Seljuc cemetery of Ahlat, with its many highly decorated tombstones.

Ahlat cemetery, Lake Van.

We next drove back to drive the southern shore, as being slightly shorter. While still on the north side, we passed a signpost to Mount Nemrut Dag. This was not the same Nemrut with the heads. It was an extinct volcano about 3,050 metres high. It was believed to have been about 4,500 metres before the last eruption, some six thousand years ago, when the whole of the top was blown off and dropped in the Van basin, blocking the old outlet and making the present lake. There were two lakes, one cold and one warm, in the crater, which had a seven-kilometre diameter. When I was up there on a previous visit, there were still snow drifts lying even though it was mid-summer and the temperature down by Lake Van was in the upper thirties (Celsius). There were also several camps of nomads who had driven some of their flocks up. Some of the children from the camp ran towards our car, throwing stones. This time, though Sinan offered to drive me up, I decided to make straight for Van, because I thought there might be time for me to climb up the old citadel before we looked for our hotel.

New Van was a couple of miles back from the lake. Old Van, which was just beside the lake, was an old Armenian town and was destroyed in 1915 in the Armenian genocide. The ruins of the citadel stood on top of a rock high above the flat land surrounding it and had a good view of the few remains of the old city and of the lake. The most well-preserved building inside the walls was a ruined mosque and medressa, but there were also ruins of an Ottoman barracks. At the bottom of the cliff, by the ticket office, there was a decent restaurant, some small shops, and a mud brick replica of an old Van house. When I came down from the top, I found a wedding party in progress, and I was immediately hauled in to join the communal dancing.

Van citadel.

While I had been up to the top of the citadel, Sinan had driven off to fill up with petrol and had taken the chance to spy out my hotel, the Tamar. This was, I am glad to say, very much better than the Batman hotel. It was smaller, spotlessly clean, and a very welcoming boutique-type hotel, situated in a side street off the crowded main boulevard and much quieter than the grander Akdamar Hotel, where I had stayed several times in the past. It was also in a very convenient position, near to the small (but excellent) museum and to a number of little restaurants and cafes.

The next day, we were to spend most of the day driving north to see Mount Ararat and the Isak Pasa Saray. The road took us along the Iranian border. Early in the holiday, we had once been briefly stopped to make sure we had no refugees from Syria on board. Now we came to an area where there were army detachments and guns on every hill top, and we were stopped again and searched much more thoroughly to make sure we were not trying to smuggle in Kurdish terrorists or weapons from Iran, for there were supposed to be terrorist training camps just across the border. When we had passed the check point, the road climbed steadily through mountainous country until we crossed a pass and suddenly saw the snow-covered top of Mount Ararat soaring up over the land below, looking almost as if it were floating in the sky. I reckon I must have been lucky over the years, for the first time I went to this area, I was warned that the chances of seeing Ararat in its full glory were very limited, for the top was almost always swathed in cloud. Each of the several times I have seen it, from both the Turkish and Armenian sides, it has been comparatively cloud free. It is an impressive mountain, reaching a little under 17,000 feet in height.

Mount Ararat.

Palace of Isak Pasa near Dogubeyazit.

The Palace of Isak Pasa was started by a local chieftain in 1685 and completed by his son, Isak Pasa, in 1784. It was situated in the foothills of Ararat, some six kilometres from the dull little frontier town of Dogubeyazit, and had wonderful views over the town and the plateau upon which the town was situated. It was the most extraordinary building, including almost every style of architecture possible at the time of its building. Later, it was used as a barracks by the Turkish army; in 1877, four hundred soldiers were quartered in the fourteen bedrooms of the Harem, and in 1917, the Russians (who were retreating from Anatolia) removed the gold-plated doors, which are now on display in the Hermitage in St Petersburg. It was recently restored to preserve the carvings, and a most inappropriate roof now covered much of the ensemble. There was also an Ottoman mosque, recently restored, a little up the hill behind the palace, as well as several other remains. On this occasion, I visited at a weekend, and there were a lot of visiting Turks on a day's outing.

Isak Pasa Palace. A view from Isak Pasa. Carving at Isak Pasa.

During the course of our return to Van, we turned off the main road for a short distance to see the Muradiye Waterfalls. The crowded car park showed how popular a place this was for visiting and picnicking. For the best view of the falls, and to reach the café, it was necessary to cross a crude and fragile-looking pedestrian suspension bridge; these bridges were popular in this area. Children seemed to love it, for they can make it sway wildly and bounce up and down, but it proved alarming to an elderly gentleman like me, and even Sinan did not seem to enjoy the crossing. Still we both traversed it in safety.

Muradiye Waterfalls. Bridge to Muradiye Waterfalls.

The next day being a Sunday, we thought it might be rather full with day trippers on Akdamar Island and so decided to leave that until the following day, my last, and we made instead for the castle at Hosap The drive up to Hosap was through fine mountainous country. The country beyond Hosap is still unknown to me, since it leads right down to the border where Iran and Iraq also meet; it was not safe to drive there until very recently, because it was the centre of Kurdish troubles. Even now, it was very heavily militarised.

Hosap was a fine castle on a steep mound situated in a small poverty-stricken village of tiny houses with flat roofs. Later in the year, these roofs were likely to be covered with haystacks, and much of the house was below ground level, which retained some warmth during the bitter winters. This form of insulation had been used since classical times, for it was mentioned by Xenephon when writing about his famous retreat with the Greek army after the death of Cyrus in 399 BC. I have been through villages in eastern Turkey a little later in the year, when the freshly cut hay was already in position. The only difference from ancient times was that some of these mud-built houses now have satellite dishes sprouting from their roofs.

We parked the car near the bridge over the river, for it was blocked to all traffic (though there must be a crossing somewhere else, for there were occasional cars on the steep track leading up to the castle entrance. When I entered, I found there was a family of Germans there, but they soon left, and the custodian and I were the only people in the building. The path inside the doorway up to the keep was also rough and steep; I suddenly remembered my previous visit with Jacynth; We had been worried when she become breathless after running to the top, until we realised that there was less oxygen at that altitude. There was a good view from the top, and one can still see the remains of the crenulated mud walls which predated the present castle; they were remarkable. The custodian, who spoke a few words of English, insisted on showing me all the different parts of the building as well as the best view points. He was also determined to make sure that I was safe and insisted on holding my arm when we encountered any rough bits, which was most of the time. At the end, he guided me carefully down back to the entrance, and I had quite a task in stopping him from accompanying me right down to the bridge. He then firmly refused to accept any tip whatsoever and said he had only done his job.

Hosap bridge and castle. View from castle of earlier mud brick walls. Hosap castle.

Halfway back towards Van, we turned off to see Cavustepe, an old Urartian palace built in the mid-700s BC on a long rocky spur looking over a plain towards some mountains; snow drifts were still visible near their tops. The most remarkable remains visible here were some beautifully dressed black stones with Urartian script incised upon them. Farther still along the road, we stopped to look at a new mosque under construction.

Cavustepe Urartian palace.

New mosque by road.

The next day, we went to see one of the finest sights near Van: the tenth-century Armenian Church of the Holy Cross on Akdamar Island. I was eager to see it again, for it had recently been restored by the Turkish government at the cost of $1.5 million. When this had been completed in 2010, there was a great ceremony, and the government allowed a Communion service to be held in the church, the first for over ninety years.

When we arrived at the ferry terminal, we were told that I would have to wait until there were enough people to make the crossing viable, so I went to the café and drank some tea, expecting a long wait, as there was no one else there. Luckily, a Japanese tour group arrived very soon, and we embarked on the twenty-minute crossing. The church, which was just visible from the mainland, had a wonderful setting, with views across the lake to magnificent mountains on the mainland, and the weather was perfect.

The restoration had been beautifully done. The frescos inside, which had been in a deplorable state, were now repaired, and in some cases, it was actually possible to make out New Testament scenes, in a pleasant, mainly blue, colour. But the real glory of the church was in the relief carvings on the exterior. There were five bands of these running right round the building; the top band, which is the smallest, shows mainly animals, and the lowest and largest shows mainly biblical scenes. My favourite was one of David with a sling and a gloating expression, confronting Goliath. Unfortunately, the angle of the sun meant I was not able to take a good photograph of him this time, but most of the reliefs were clearly visible.

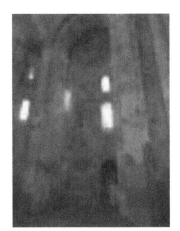 

Armenian Church of the Holy Cross, Akdamar Island, Lake Van.

Lake Van from Akdamar Island.

After our return to Van, I took quite a long walk round the whole spur upon which the citadel stood and was able to see what little remained of the old city. It was a suitable end to an enjoyable and most interesting holiday.

A few months after my return, a large earthquake devastated Van and killed nearly seven hundred people, though damage to the citadel and to the church on Akdamar Island was minimal. Apparently, the church was built with smaller stones at a lower level and larger above, which helped it withstand the quake.

CHAPTER 9

GEORGIA: A FORMER RUSSIAN REPUBLIC FULL OF ACTIVE CHURCHES

Carving on fortified church at Ananuri.

Among the Christmas cards I received in 2010 was one from Roger Peers, an old friend who used to be curator of the Dorchester Museum. He wrote in it, "I hope to be going to Georgia next year." I immediately phoned him up to find out with whom he was travelling, for I had been trying to arrange a trip there with Bath Travel for some time. So it was that I took my last trip of 2011 to Georgia on a tour with Eastern Approaches. Unfortunately, the proprietor of the firm, Warwick Ball, who had been going to lead the tour himself, had to go into hospital, but he found a very able replacement in Beatrice Tessier, who though she had never led a tour before, had written an excellent book called *Russian Frontiers*, about eighteenth-century British travellers in the Caspian, Caucasus, and Central Asian regions.

I drove up to Heathrow, where I was booked in the Holiday Inn. When I arrived there, I found the hotel I had reached was the wrong hotel, for there were two Holiday Inns at

Heathrow: one in Sipson Road and the other in Sipson Way. When I reached the correct hotel, I found the person booking in next to me had made the same mistake, the other way round, and was just being sent to the first one. The next morning, on the coach to the airport, I found myself talking to someone who had done exactly the same as me. Anyway, the bed was comfortable and the food good.

The flight the next day did something I had never experienced before: it arrived in Tbilisi over an hour and a half early. This meant that our coach had not arrived, and Beatrice found that the Georgian office had closed for the night, so we had quite a long wait. Still it gave us time to have a meal and to change some money. In order to change a fifty US dollar note, I had to provide my passport and to sign four different documents. When we reached the hotel, we found that all the rooms, on whatever floor, started with the number "3". We also found that what we called the ground floor, they called the first floor, all of which caused some confusion.

Jvari Church, overlooking city of Mtskheta.

The next morning, we left in two minibuses for the sixth-century Jvari church, on a hill overlooking the former capital Mtskheta. We were accompanied by a Georgian guide, Lela, who was to stay with us for the whole of our trip. Beatrice and she seemed to get on well with each other (after some early difficulties). This church had no frescos but several good outside carvings (some of which we could not see, since they were covered for restoration).

We had plenty of time to explore this building before we were driven down to see the eleventh-century Sveti Tskhoveli Cathedral in Mtskheta, built on the foundations of a huge fifth-century stone basilica. The dome of this church was covered with scaffolding, and we were to find that there was a very great restoration programme under way, as well as a lot of new church building throughout Georgia which proved to be the most religious country I have ever visited. The churches were nearly always full of people of all ages, and in the countryside, everyone passing a church tended to make the sign of the cross. Unlike Jvari, the cathedral was full of frescos, many of them dating from the sixteenth and seventeenth centuries, though some painted in the nineteenth century were painted along the lines of old eleventh-century work.

Sveti Tskhoveli Cathedral, Mtskheta. Fresco in cathedral.

After lunch, we were taken to the Church of St Nino at Santavro. St Nino is the patron saint of Georgia; there are many legends about her. According to one version, she was a cousin of our own patron St George, and he was indeed much revered in Georgia, hence the country's name. She for quite a long time was supposed to have lived under a bramble bush to save herself from persecution. On another occasion, she was given a branch of a vine tree, which she fashioned into a cross, tying it with her own hair, which was not strong enough to hold the arms of the cross at right angles to the stem, and they drooped, so in many Georgian churches, the cross of St Nino is still displayed with its arms slanted downwards. While being held as a prisoner, she cured Queen Nana of a bad illness, as a result of which Nana became a Christian. Later, King Mirian was also converted, and Georgia became a Christian country in the year AD 303, only two years after Armenia, the first country to adopt Christianity. From both this eleventh-century church and from the cathedral, there was a good view of Jvari church, standing on its steep hill. Another miracle St Nino was involved in was in the building of the first church in Mtskheta. When the foundations were finished, three wooden pillars were cut from a cedar tree which had grown from the grave of Sidonia, the sister of King Elias, who had been buried with part of Christ's crucifixion robe on the site of where the new church was to be erected. The first two pillars went in without any trouble, but the third just hovered in the air and could not be lowered, whatever methods were used. Then St Nino went to the church by herself one night and lowered the pillar upright into its correct position.

The Church of St Nino was now run by nuns who do not allow any photography inside the building. Outside in the grounds, there was a separate belfry and a tiny little chapel which was said to have been built by St Nino herself, though I suspect the evidence for this was not very strong.

The lunch we had in a local restaurant had continual new courses arriving in a style typical of Lebanon. In fact, the food we had for the whole trip was of a very high standard and similar in style to the Lebanese and the Turkish. The red wine served was always excellent, though the white varied in standard.

Near Santavro, there was a Bronze Age cemetery, covering a large area and holding several other remains as well as tombs.

Church of St Nino, Mtskheta. Bronze Age cemetery, Mtskheta.

We also took an hour's drive on an unsurfaced road up into the mountains to see the church of Shiomgvine, built in the sixth century over the grave of a Syrian monk; it was in a spectacular position below some cliffs.

Shiomgvine church.

We used the same two minibuses on the next day's trip. Unfortunately, the track down to the twelfth-century church of Betania was so bad that after quite a long drive, it became obvious that four-wheel drive was really needed; we dismounted and had to walk the remaining distance, more than a mile. The track was very skiddy, and at one point I slipped and fell on my back. Luckily, I escaped with a few grazes on my hand, unlike someone else, who damaged his knee in his fall. Several others in the party also had narrow escapes from falling. We passed the first minibus, which had also stopped to unload its passengers, about a hundred yards farther on and watched it trying to turn around.

The church itself was well worth a visit and contained some good frescos, including one of the very few known portraits of the famous Georgian Queen Tamar. Unfortunately, no photography was allowed inside the church. There was a service on all the time we were there, and one side of the church was being used for Communion and the other for blessings. A lot of incense was being used, and at one point the doors of the iconostasis were opened so that we could see that part of the church. Outside in the churchyard was a small spring with some delightful (if rather naïve) carvings on it.

Betania church, in the mountains.

Carving on Betania spring.

When we were due to return to the minibuses, Lela managed to arrange for the majority of us to be given a lift up in a four-wheel-drive people carrier. We then regained the main road, also unmade up, but with a better surface, and carried on, stopping en route for a picnic lunch on the way to our next visit, the church of Manglisi. Though this was the second-oldest church in Bulgaria, it had been much altered over the years, and the frescos were hidden under whitewash, so the building said little to most of us, even though it was situated in a lovely mountain valley, and the local village had a number of attractive, if run-down, houses.

Manglisi church.

Old house near Manglisi church.

On our return to Tbilisi, we stopped by an excellent bookshop, where I bought a book on Georgian art, which I had been tempted by in Mtskheta and was pleased to find here at less than three-quarters of the price. I then joined some of the others for tea in the attractive open air café attached to the shop.

We had supper in a noisy tourist restaurant, which featured an awful display of dancing. However, the food was good, and the people at the table next to us presented us with a flagon of even better wine than we had been consuming.

Our next day was to be a long one, as we set off in two coaches to stay for two nights in the little town of Akhaltsikhe, deep in the Lesser Caucasus, with several visits on the way. We stopped first at the eleventh-century church of Samtivisi. My only other visit here, many years before, had left me slightly disappointed in the proportions of the church, for the drum of the dome seemed too high for the rest of the building. I still felt that but decided that this apparent deficiency on the outside was more than made up for by the superb exterior carvings. Inside, one had a marvellous impression of soaring space up into the dome, and there were substantial remains of frescos, some dating from the eleventh century.

Samtivisi church.

Outside, the delightful little domed gatehouse was partly covered with scaffolding and being restored. The area around the church was being excavated, and the foundations of a second church, of a similar size, had been discovered, right beside (and possibly even touching) the present building. There was a striking modern tomb of a wrestler who was described, in Georgian and English, as having been the champion of the world and who had apparently died young in some accident.

After we left Samtivisi, we drove through the town of Gori, notorious as the birthplace of Stalin. After he died, a museum was made near where he was born; the citizens remained proud of the local boy made good, so much so that the statue of him erected in Stalin Square stood for many years as the only remaining statue of him in the whole of the old Soviet Union. I actually saw it on my previous visit here; it was not removed until 2010, when the authorities decided they had had enough of Russia after the conflict of 2008 and pulled it down.

We did not stop at Gori but travelled on the few miles to see the ancient cave city of Uplitsikhe. This town was a trading centre from at least the fifth century BC and was still being lived in by monks in the thirteenth century AD. The entrance was a very steep and rough scramble up over rocks to reach the town. Lela had obviously foreseen that some of us might find difficulty with this path and had enlisted a local to help any of us who needed it. Several were glad of his help, but I found myself able to scale the heights while he was helping others. There were the remains of very many cave buildings including a small theatre, a wine store, a most remarkable pharmacy, churches, and halls. At the very top was a small chapel, which I had assumed on my previous visit to be modern, but I now found dated from the ninth century. The way out took us down through an eighty-metre-long tunnel which had been built for water carriers from the river. Much of the place needed urgent repair if it was to survive many more years. Places like this need as much care as is given to the churches.

Cave city of Uplitsikhe, near Gori.

Ninth-century chapel, Uplitsikhe.

Until we went to Uplitsikhe, our visits had all been to churches, but from now on, although churches were still to play a major part in our itinerary, there was to be a much greater variety in what we saw. We now drove back through Gori to another church, Atenis Sione, which I was particularly looking forward to seeing, since when Jacynth and I had tried to visit it, we had only been able to view it from a distance, since the key holder was away. Even this visit was not perfect, for much of it was under scaffolding, and we could only see a little of the exterior decoration. But we were able to see the early frescos; they were very fine but very faded and needed expert work done on them, which, judging by the other churches we saw, was likely to happen soon. Unfortunately, photography was not permitted inside, nor were there any postcards. I can understand when they do not allow photography, but many of these churches could add to their funds by the sale of cards. As we left, a visiting priest emerged, stuffing his mouth full of the grapes he had plucked from the vines growing in the church grounds.

Atenis Sione Church, near Gori.   *Sculpture in Borjoni Spa.*

We ate trout freshly taken from the restaurant's own pond, before setting off on the road to Akhaltsikhe. We were delayed for a time by a puncture but eventually reached the spa town of Borjoni, where we stopped for a time and several of the party took the waters. I declined, after hearing some of their comments on the taste, and contented myself with taking a photograph of a modern sculpture. The drive on was not far, and we settled in to our fairly basic but clean hotel, which also provided good food for our evening meal. It was at this meal that I discovered that two of our party knew friends of mine in Sherborne, and a third had been married to the daughter of one of my father's best friends. The mini bar in my room was empty, and even if it had been well stocked, there was no place where it could have been plugged.

The next day started with a threatening sky, and it looked as if it was going to rain, but suddenly the sky cleared and we had a fine sunny day, not too hot. For our trip, we were packed into four 4WD vehicles, since we were told, rightly, the roads were not good. Our first stop, well up in the hills, was to see the ruins of the tenth-century Khertvisi castle, standing high above the road. We were told that it was not worth our climbing up because there was nothing at all left inside of the magnificent walls. However, all of us made our way across the river, by a very rickety foot bridge, in order to get an even better view. We then drove on through wild countryside to see the main object of the day's trip, the cave monastery, frequently called the cave city, of Vardzia, overlooking the river.

Khertvisi castle.

Cave monastery, Vardzia.

This complex was probably started by King George in 1156 and consecrated as a monastery in 1185 by his daughter, Queen Tamar. Its over 600 caves in many tiers housed some two thousand monks, until an earthquake in 1283 sliced away the face of the cliff, and further quakes and attacks, first by a Persian army and then by the Turks, reduced it to its present state. However, much remained, some of it in a good state of preservation. The main church still displayed some fine frescos, including one of Queen Tamar herself. The bell tower, with fine views of the valley, marked the entrance into the monastery, a refectory, wine depot, and hall, not to speak of numerous cells, living quarters, and other rooms. Since this was a border area, it was closed off during the Russian occupation. However, a few monks had re-established themselves in some of the cave cells, and one could see, from a small distance, that they had made themselves quite comfortable, for I was able to spot a sofa in one, a vase of flowers in another, and even a television disc in yet another. I doubted that they lived there during the winter, for it must often be cut off from the outer world, and water would be a problem, since the original irrigation channels no longer existed.

Vardzia cave monastery.

Chapel in Vardzia.

We had lunch at a café set in an attractive garden under a tent roof but with open sides, so we could admire the river view while eating trout on skewers and drinking a very good red wine, produced by the owner himself from his own grapes.

The next lap of our journey needed the 4WD vehicles. We had returned for the greater part of our outward journey when we turned off the main road onto a much narrower, steeper, and even worse surfaced track, which wound up and up into the mountains, the surface deteriorating the whole time. It took us thirty-five minutes to cover the six or seven kilometres to reach our destination, the Sapara Monastery, in a lovely wooded valley. Then we descended from the vehicles at a view point and unanimously decided to walk the remaining half mile on foot.

Sapara Monastery.

Despite the difficult journey, the trip to Sapara Monastery proved very well worthwhile. The monastery included several churches, the oldest of which, the tenth-century Church of the Dormition, had a beautiful altar screen. The main church now was the late thirteenth— to early fourteenth-century Church of St Sabbas, which had some good frescos. The exterior carvings on several of the buildings were worthy of note. After the drive back to Akhaltsikhe, we spent a little time visiting the small but attractive covered bazaar, selling mainly fruit and vegetables. Beatrice delayed our supper by giving us a talk, to the annoyance of some of the staff, who were waiting to serve us a good meal with fine red wine.

The next day, we set off for Batumi in our four vehicles; the road was good, apart from continual delays due to cows and calves, which anywhere in Georgia seemed to have right of way and wandered in numbers, without any human attendants, all over the road. We then turned off onto a track to cover several miles, after which we turned onto an even worse track, to see the early fourteenth-century monastery of Zarzma. Here, once again, we found extensive restoration work in progress. Despite this, we were able to have a good view of the attractive church and churchyard, with some primitive tombstones made of tufa as well as a large number of beehives tended by the monks, some of whom were engaged in helping with the work in progress. Inside the church were some remarkable frescos dating from the fourteenth to the sixteenth centuries, as well as some pillars with very naïve carvings on them.

Zarzma monastery.

We now returned to the first track and assumed we would soon rejoin the main road. This, however, proved to be the main road, and we drove up over a high pass for some ninety kilometres before hitting a surfaced road again. We saw a number of interesting minarets beside a river down in the valley below us. Soon after reaching the valley, we turned off onto yet another rough track, which was to take us to a small church. Neither Lela nor Beatrice had seen this church before, nor had any of the drivers, and it took us an hour from turning off before we reached the little church of Skhalto to find that it was not so much being restored as rebuilt, added to which it was very firmly locked. Lela was eventually able to find a workman with a key so we were able to get in. The inside had also been mainly stripped out, and the frescos that survived seemed, with few exceptions, too far gone for any meaningful repair. There was a strong feeling among the group that the two-hour round trip from the main road had not been worthwhile. In fact, this detour meant we would not reach Batumi in time to see the Roman fort of Gonio, down the coast of the Black Sea. Luckily, Beatrice and Lela decided that there would be time to visit it the next day, before we left Batumi on our journey up into the Caucasus Mountains.

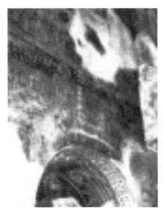

Skhalto church.   *Skhalto church.*   *Batumi sea front sculpture.*

The hotel in Batumi was a welcomed surprise to me. It was named Intourist Palace, and every Intourist hotel I had visited in the past had been a concrete monstrosity built by the communists; the word "Palace" usually indicated anything but. This one, however, had been restored in 2006 and really was palatial. It was separated from the sea front by a small park, and there was time before we went out for supper to take a walk along the sea front, with attractive modern statues, and see the sun set over the Black Sea. We had an excellent meal at a sea-view restaurant, and I found that one of our party was a pupil at Bournemouth School for Girls at the time that Jacynth was teaching there (though she had not been taught by her).

The weather forecast for the next day was for heavy rain, but in fact the sky was clear and the day remained sunny. It proved useful having four vehicles, for some of the group did not want to start early, so they were able to sleep on while the rest of us rose fairly early to see the Roman fort at Gonio, which had some of the best-preserved Roman walls of any legionary fortress, each of them about two hundred metres long. Some excavations inside had uncovered the extensive remains of water pipes and the foundations of other buildings, and there was a small museum, but it mostly consisted of flowers and fruit trees.

Gonio Roman fort, Batumi. Walls at Gonio Roman fort. Water pipes at Gonio.

A fine gold treasure, which was excavated in 1974, was now in a museum in Tbilisi. The disciple Matthias, the thirteenth apostle of Jesus, who was chosen after the death of Judas Iscariot, was supposed to have been buried here, and a cross had been erected in his memory (though the burial place had not yet been discovered). As we left the fort, the rest of the party arrived, and we drove on along the coast to the cliff-top fort of Tsikhisdziri, the site of the ancient Roman fortress of Petra. This was an attractive little fortress with fine views out over the sea, and we spent half an hour wandering round the remains. We then turned inland and drove over flat country, but approaching the mountains, till we stopped for lunch at the remote town of Zugidi. Here, I was very surprised to be greeted by a call of "Hello, Dermot." It proved to be Tom and his wife Jenny, who had travelled in Albania with me two years previously. They were going in the opposite direction to us and had just been saying to their companions that they had never yet met anyone they knew on any of their travels.

We had been warned that the next part of our journey through the mountains would probably take at least four to five hours, because the road was so bad. In fact, it took far less since the road past a lovely green reservoir and then up through a magnificent gorge to the town of Mestia, where we were to stay for two nights, had recently been surfaced, so although it was still very windy, steep, and narrow, it was a smooth drive with magnificent views of snow-covered mountain peaks, over 5,000 metres high.

Mestia itself was an extraordinary town with a large number of tower houses. Every other house was either being demolished or rebuilt, because the place was being turned into a ski resort. What it will be like with the very narrow windy road full of traffic I dare not think, since there were many places it was not wide enough for two vehicles to pass each other. The streets in Mestia itself were none of them made up and were full of cattle, bulls, and pigs. We were told the main Tamar street would soon be surfaced. Our own hotel was still uncompleted and had some very odd plumbing arrangements. My shower had no surround at all; the water just fell onto the flat bathroom floor, for there was no shower tray. Outside, the marble stairs to my first-floor room had no rail and an open drop to the ground below. My bathroom light went off, but by the time I found someone to come and look at it, it had come on again. After supper, it went off again but came on once more after a couple of minutes. We had a good meal with a very rough red wine, so I was extra careful when going back to my room in the dark.

The mountain resort of Mestia.

The next day at breakfast, we found a noisy group of Israeli walkers, also staying at the hotel, fortifying themselves with vodka before starting on their day's trek. We ourselves had only about thirty miles to travel to reach our destination, Ushguli, possibly at 2,200 metres the highest all-year-round-inhabited village in Europe. This short distance, however, took us nearly three hours' driving time, even in our 4WD vehicles, such was the state of the so-called road. It started not too badly, though not surfaced, but as soon as we turned off the main road and started climbing steeply into the mountains, the road surface became almost undriveable. We had two stops on the way, the first a photo stop for the view, and the second in a minute hamlet called Nakipari. Here, the tiny but tall Church of St George, built in 1130, had untouched and unrestored frescos from the same date; its east end exterior boasted some wonderful bosses built above a pagan altar. It was very dark inside the church, and no flash photography was allowed, but it was still possible to discern the frescos.

Nakipari church.

The road further on was even worse and, according to my guide book, was open only from April until December. We arrived in the village of Ushguli, one of the most primitive places I have ever visited. These pictures are in the main street.

The main street, Ushguli village.

The only driveable road did not go into the village itself but acted as a type of bypass, cutting through between two parts of the village and leading up to the high point, where there was little but a tiny barnlike church, a tower house and a magnificent view down the valley to the village proper and also up into the mountains (partly cloud covered when we were there). We had a picnic at this high point before driving down, dismounting, and walking along the muddy and dung-covered rough high street, stopping at a tiny café and shop for some refreshment and another view before carrying on down to where there was a small ethnographic museum in one of the many tower houses which dated from the Middle Ages and were anything from four to six storeys high. The museum had a fine collection of gold and silver icons, which were reached by climbing up the very steep and narrow stairs.

Ushguli village.

By pure chance a year earlier, I had met a Georgian staying with a friend of mine near my home who had lived in this village for a time. He described the winter as hellish, with no road contact with the outside world and so cold that when he went to bed, he did not undress but put on six layers of clothing. Television was available when the electricity was working but otherwise people there lived much as they had done for hundreds of years.

There was a sudden downpour while we were in the museum. Fortunately, it stopped in time for us to return to our cars before starting again, just after we had boarded them. Luckily, the rain did not last for long, since there were several places where streams flowed across the road; the water had risen since our outward journey, and the drivers were obviously worried that we might be stranded if it continued.

The next day, we drove back down the road from Mestia. It was mainly dry, though the mountains were now enveloped in cloud and some fog. When we reached the level, we drove along roads often lined with small Uzbek Soviet-style houses and gardens, until we reached the ruins of the fortress of Nokalakevi, which had been destroyed by the Arabs in the ninth century AD. The walls were very fine, and there were a few buildings inside as well as a church. There was also a tunnel down to the river below. Excavations were taking place, and one of the team came out and gave us a brief history. It rained a little while we were in the castle, but luckily the heavy shower delayed until we were lunching in the café across the road. It then remained dry for our visit to Vani. Here, we first saw the museum with artefacts dating from pre-Christian times. The treasury was then unlocked for us to inspect the magnificent golden objects stored there. The site itself, which was reached by another swaying bridge, was not as interesting as the museum. It had been destroyed and burnt in 100 BC, and there were few ruins visible.

We finally drove to Kutaisi, near which our pleasant hotel was situated in a woodland setting.

The next day started cloudy, and rain was forecast, but the clouds soon cleared, and we had a fine sunny day. We exchanged our 4WD cars for a mini coach for the rest of the trip. This proved rather crowded, and after two days, another smaller bus was added to our transport, which we also kept for the remainder of our journey.

Our next trip was to Nikortsminda Church, which involved a steep climb; in one town a lorry just behind us became stuck under a low bridge. Luckily, by the time of our return, it had been extricated. We had been warned that this church was under restoration and that we would probably not be able to get inside, but we also heard it would still be worth visiting for the exterior decorative carving. Indeed the stonework was the best I had ever seen, different from (but to me even more pleasing than) that at Akdamar near Van in Turkey. The surrounding ground was bare, having been dug up, we were told, for a new garden.

Nikortsminda Church, near Kutaisi.

However, the greatest joy of this trip was the fact that it was a Sunday and the church was open for a service, so we were able to enter. The inside was full of wooden scaffolding and lit only by candles, which allowed just enough light to catch glimpses of the frescos, which covered the walls and the dome. A choir of women, all dressed in black, made a most beautiful sound. We were there for a part of the service when the iconostasis was opened for a time, and we could see the priest dressed in the most marvellous rich robes, conducting the celebration. All the time, as is the custom in Orthodox services, the congregation was coming and going, but it was obvious that the people really felt that they were celebrating something of the greatest importance, and the way they had to dodge and duck the scaffolding all added to the emotional feel. It was the most magical service I had ever attended, and I wish I could have stayed on much longer.

We next retraced our steps to visit Bagrat Cathedral, which overlooked Kutaisi from the top of a steep hill. I had heard that only the foundations of this building were now visible, since it had been blown up by the Turks in 1691 during military operations. However, we found that it was in the process of being completely rebuilt according to the original plan, and when this has been completed in 2022, it will once again dominate the town. It was already a most imposing building.

Bagrat Cathedral, Kutaisi.

After lunch, we drove a few miles out of Kutaisi to visit the Gelati Monastery, a complex of three churches on a hillside. On the way there, overhead gas pipes were visible in the villages, painted yellow as they had been in Bukhara in Uzbekistan. Once again, one of the buildings was swathed in scaffolding. The main cathedral, however, was a fine piece of architecture, with excellent frescos inside, dating from the twelfth to the seventeenth centuries. It was a very spacious church so that two baptisms and a wedding were able to take place simultaneously, while several other wedding groups were queuing up outside to take their turns.

Gelati Monastery near Kutaisi.   *Wedding at Gelati.*   *Inside Gelati Monastery.*

On our return to Kutaisi, we had an hour during which we had time to explore what proved to be a delightful town with an attractive church, a fine opera house, an attractive market, several other good buildings, and a pleasant little park, before being driven back to our hotel. I even managed to change some money at a reasonable rate without all the red tape I had had at the airport exchange.

The next day, we had a long drive to Gudauri up in the high Caucasus Mountains. We started under a clear blue sky and arrived at the Mountain Hut Hotel in a chilly mist. Near the start, there were extensive stalls selling pottery and other goods, and we stopped to visit one. Later on, we stopped at another stall, of which there were several on the road, selling a type of large mushroom for which the region was well known.

Stalls on road from Kutaisi to Gori.

Much of the countryside was fine agricultural valley. We once again found ourselves near Gori and stopped for another excellent trout meal at the same restaurant as before. After lunch, we drove up the Georgian Military Highway. There was not much traffic on this road, since the Russian border crossing to which it led was closed. On the way, we visited the fortified church at Ananuri, overlooking a reservoir. The main seventeenth-century church, one of three, had some excellent exterior carvings as well as a few remains of interior frescos.

Fortified church at Ananuri.

From this time on, the road climbed into the mountains, and the final twenty kilometres were very steep. The road surface deteriorated rapidly, since this road, which had once been the main highway to the USSR, now led to a dead end when it reached the frontier. Nevertheless, it was a beautiful drive. Gudauri was a tiny mountain village destined, we were told, to become a winter sports centre and consisting almost entirely of hotels (not that there were many even of these). Our own hotel was small but spotlessly clean, and the water was almost too hot. Its position was excellent, with good views down the valley through which we had driven and up to the pass of nearly 2,400 metres, over which we were to drive the next day. Several of us took the chance to stretch our legs with a walk to where a new church, still under construction, was standing on a ridge, with a beautiful view which we could see even in the mist. It never failed to amaze me how many new churches were being built and old ones repaired throughout the whole country. There seemed to be no doubt that there was a tremendous religious enthusiasm, among young and old, since their freedom from the old Soviet Union. The evening meal was again excellent; indeed, the food we had throughout our trip could seldom be faulted and was almost up to the standard of the food in Lebanon, which I had always put at the top of my list.

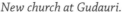

New church at Gudauri.   *View from Gudauri church.*

We started the next day in thick fog, which started clearing as we drove down from the pass over an appalling road surface and, at one point, under a long anti-avalanche tunnel. There were several of these tunnels, most of them closed and bypassed by the track. We stopped at one point where the water running down the mountainside had chemicals in it, which caused a very large orange-coloured build-up. There was a disgusting sulphuric smell, and we were told that the spa-type water was good for you to drink, but that it had a horrible taste. By the side of the road, there was an array of wooden poles and bars which looked as though they were intended for some kind of pagan worship. However, just before we drove off, a van drew up which unloaded several women who proceeded to cover the bars with various forms of clothing, which they hoped to sell to any of the few passers-by.

Orange chemical water deposit.   *Setting up roadside stalls.*

We then drove on down into the valley, the fog entirely disappearing and giving us lovely views of the mountains, some of them snow covered. We stopped for a short time at the frontier village of Karbezi, from where there was a particularly remarkable view of a peak over 5,000 metres high, and a church of St George framed on a high ridge in front of it. The road from here to the Russian frontier was suddenly beautifully surfaced. We dismounted at the frontier and were allowed to walk around, but photography was forbidden. Just by the frontier there was a new church, officially opened by the president only a week before our visit. We were told that the reason for this church was that the Russians had been gradually pushing the frontier forward, yard by yard, into Georgian territory, and this was to mark a point that was indisputably Georgian and would stop further advances. I sneaked an illegal photograph of this church from the coach window as we started on our return journey back up the pass.

Frontier village of Karbezi.

Church within yards of Russian frontier.

This was another area where the gas pipes ran above the ground. One was visible just in front of the church. Once back over the pass, it became cloudy and remained so for the rest of the day. At one point on our journey down, we passed a car going the other way, travelling very slowly with its hazard warning lights on and towing a donkey behind it.

Our next visit was to a nunnery called Ninotsminda. The original church was a ruin as the result of earthquakes in 1824 and 1848, but the original walls, for it had been a fortified place, were still in a very good state of preservation, and several of the other old buildings, particularly the bell tower with its magnificent brickwork (revealing a Safavid-Persian influence), were in good condition. There were also in the grounds a large number of flower beds with a large display of different species of flowers in them. This reminded me of Romania, where you could always tell whether a complex was run by nuns or monks, for the nuns always grew flowers but the monks ignored them.

The guesthouse at Telavi, where we were to spend the next two nights, was an extraordinary place of several buildings. My magnificent wardrobe was full of family clothing and other personal belongings. There was no lock to the door, and the bathroom and loo, for there was no en-suite, had a bolt that did not function. Luckily, there were two lots of facilities for three rooms, and the two ladies on the same floor agreed to use one and I the other. But it was a very comfortable and characterful place, very clean, and we believed the owners when they said they had never had the need to use keys, for there was never any crime in the town.

Ninotsminda nunnery.

We were to have another church visiting day from Telavi. The first was to Gremi, the tiny former hilltop capital of the Kingdom of Kakheti, consisting of a fortified church and tower house. Here there was another service, this time with a male choir, for it was the birthday of the Virgin Mary. Again the church was very full, although it was not a Sunday. We then drove past fields, often filled with yellow daisies, to the monastery of Nekresi, on a much higher hill, with its own minibus service to the top for those who did not want a thirty-minute slog, with buildings dating from the fourth to the sixteenth centuries. One of its churches was having its frescos restored. There was also a very large room where wine had been both made and stored.

Nekresi monastery.

Our first trip after lunch was to the stupendous early eleventh-century cathedral of Alaverdi. My only disappointment with this was the fact that photography was not only not permitted in the church itself but also anywhere within the walls. The church had several times been damaged by earthquakes, and the inside was white washed in the mid-nineteenth century, so the frescos were hidden (though restoration in 1967 revealed some of the old paintings). Much restoration was going on both in the church and the other buildings within the old fortifications.

Alaverdi cathedral.

Our final visit was to the old monastery of Ikalto, where they had the largest area for treading grapes in the whole of Georgia (which seems to say something about the monks' drinking habits). The view of the church was also improved by tall Cyprus trees, which we did not see anywhere else in the country. Some of the walls of the church had unrepaired earthquake cracks in them, which made parts of the structure look rather unsafe.

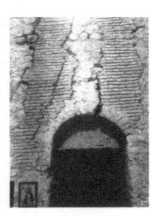

Ikalto monastery.   *Grape treading area.*   *Earthquake cracks.*

We returned to Telavi in plenty of time for me to take a walk around the delightful small town, where there were many fine old houses and a museum, which we were to visit the next day before leaving. I also visited another attractive church where, although there was no service going on, a large number of people, mostly young, were going in and out to say personal prayers. At supper that evening, there was a surprise, for it was the birthday of one of the party, so in addition to the usual excellent food and wine, we had Georgian champagne and a birthday cake.

The next morning, we had a little free time before the museum opened, and I explored the area of Telavi near our guest house. Several of the old houses had shops with small windows with something such as a shoe hanging outside to demonstrate their trade rather than any writing on a board or lintel. Then we went first to visit the museum inside the defensive walls, which was the palace of the much-revered King Erakli II, whose fine mounted statue stood outside the main gate. The outside of the main building was very shabby and needed urgent repair, though the inside was well kept. It was interesting to see the king's bath house, which was situated at a considerable distance from the main building.

Cobbler's shop, Telavi.   *Statue of King Erakli II.*   *Bath house of King Erakli II.*

Our next visit was to the attractive home of the poet Alexander Chavchavadze, which had been turned to a museum. The tour started with a drink of the white wine brewed on the estate, which proved to be quite the best white wine we met in the whole of our trip to Georgia. The rooms in the house were fine, but the old Babushka, a very grim-looking lady, kept a very beady looking eye on us to make sure we did not misbehave in any way while doing the tour.

We were then driven to the lovely two-domed church of Khelatsminda, the only two-domed church in the country, we were told. This was set in woods, and we had to walk half a kilometre down a steep track to reach it (though on my previous visit, Jacynth and I had driven right down to the building). One monk sat outside, with a dog and some empty *pithoi*, speaking the whole time on a mobile phone while his companion guarded the inside, only coming out as we were leaving. When I said good-bye and thanked them, they both stood up, smiled, and bowed to me.

Museum of poet Alexander Chavchavadze. *Church of Kelatsminda.*

We then drove to the walled little city of Sighnaghi, whose walls were supposed to be very long and complete. But we drove right into the centre of the very attractive town without seeing any walls. Where were the famous walls? We eventually discovered that the walls just ran along one side of the town and then turned outwards to enclose a large valley, filled mainly with woodland and hardly any dwellings at all. In fact, the city was outside the walls. I have never seen anything like this anywhere else.

We lunched at a restaurant in the centre square of the city before moving on to an attractive hotel in the same square, after which we were free to explore individually. I went first to the nearby museum which had recently been restored. There I met Roger Peers the former curator of the Dorchester Museum, who told me he thought it was one of the best-arranged museums he had ever seen. There were some lovely ancient artefacts and a few good pictures in the gallery, including *The Procuress* by Cranach. There was a marvellous view from the museum over the plain, though due to the heat haze, it was only just possible to make out the outline of the Caucasus Mountains.

City of Sighnaghi.

I then walked through a city gate in the walls to find I had left the city and was in the large wooded valley, with very lengthy walls surrounding it. After a time in this wall-enclosed valley, I returned through the gate and explored the city itself. One of the churches was completely new and attractive, though not as fine as another old church, with a remarkable belfry down by the city walls. There were also many good nineteenth-century houses and an attractive fountain. Our own hotel had by its entrance an old penny farthing-type tricycle which had been converted into a plant holder, an imaginative bit of recycling. Altogether, Sighnaghi was a good place to spend our last night before returning to Tbilisi for our final two nights.

Hotel entrance, Sighnaghi.

Sighnaghi walls and tower.

Sighnaghi museum.

Much of our journey back to Tbilisi was taken up by a visit to the fortified and part cave monastery of David Gareja. The whole complex, in fact, consisted of a large number of monasteries stretching for many kilometres along a mountain ridge, overlooking Azerbaijan on one side. The road to the main buildings had deteriorated since my only previous visit and now really should only be visited by 4WD vehicles, though our two mini coaches just made it. The journey was complicated even more by being full of cattle and sheep in several places, this time attended by men mounted on horseback, driving them down from their summer pastures. We were also delayed by a film crew setting up their equipment near our destination. Otherwise, the country was bleak and dreary for many miles except for one desolate village set up by the Soviets in the 1970s, for three villages were destroyed by avalanches in the Caucasus area. This village was now nearly deserted, for many of its inhabitants had returned to their beloved mountains, so different from this bleak semi-desert plain. The main buildings of the monastery, the Lavra, were situated at the very end of the road. This was now, once again, a working monastery, and on my previous visit, one of the monks suddenly recognised our driver as an old school friend and embraced him warmly. In general, these monks do not really enjoy visitors, and we were only allowed into a part of the building. The old path up above to the Udabno cave monastery, with the best frescos, may only be used by the monks themselves, and the path up to them from outside the buildings, which apparently takes over half an hour each way, is, to say the least of it, narrow, rough, steep, and slippery. I regret to say that after one look at it I joined the greater number of our party who decided not to try it. Indeed, one of the more active and younger members of our party who did start up gave up after only some twenty metres and slithered down again. However, it was still worth the visit; the line of the monks' cave cells stretching up the hillside was very impressive, as was the watch tower. Also of interest, outside the complex, was the carved water channel, which still carried water from the winter rains down to a semi-covered cistern.

When our climbers returned, we found a flattish area on the hillside not far from the buildings to sit and have our picnic lunch before taking the long track back to rejoin the main road back to Tbilisi.

We arrived with plenty of time before supper, and I took a walk near our hotel and discovered the ruins of a large and what must have been impressive church, which had been destroyed in an earthquake only a few years before; it looked as though much of what remained would also soon collapse. I vaguely remembered it whole and unblemished from my previous visit.

David Gareja monastery.

Our final day in Tbilisi was to be an interesting one. Since the museums did not open until eleven, I had time for a further walk before we met our coaches. Just near to our hotel was the thirteenth-century Metekhi Church, with wonderful views across the Mtkvari River to the Narikala fortress and with a fine modern equestrian statue of Vakhtang Gorgasili in its grounds. This church replaced an earlier fifth-century temple and underwent many changes over the years; recently, it was used as a youth theatre before being restored for worship. The porch was under the by-now-familiar wooden scaffolding; however, I was able to go inside, where it was plain but pleasing.

I then walked down the hill, crossed the river, and had a look at the bath houses and mosque with its tiled front, where both Sunnis and Shias worship together, and near them the Armenian church.

Metekhi church, Tbilisi.   *Tbilisi mosque.*

I returned in time to join our coach for the tour, first to the Icon Museum. There was some sort of meeting for senior clergy taking place when we arrived. As they left, one of the most resplendent marched up to our group and, to his great surprise, shook the hand of one of our members. Afterwards, we decided it was because he was the only member of our party who sported a beard. The treasury of the Icon Museum was unlocked to allow only ten people in at a time (plus a museum guide, who rattled off her stuff without any feeling, and a female guard to make sure we all kept together). I was glad I was with the first group, for the next lot had to wait for over half an hour before we were through. I was glad to see again the marvellous Khakhuli Triptych, which had originated in Ha Ho Church in Turkey.

We next had coffee in the Marriot Hotel and watched the start of the France versus New Zealand rugby match before walking to a new museum which contained, among other exhibits, wonderful gold artefacts, many of them from Vani; all of them were beautifully exhibited, and we were free to walk round by ourselves.

After a good lunch, we were free, and I spent nearly three hours exploring. Among the places I visited was the Kashveti Church of St George, a large building built in the early 1900s to replace a sixth-century church, which had to be demolished as unsafe. This was very busy indeed where a bishop, one of those we had seen at the Icon Museum, was conducting a wedding while several other brides-to-be were queuing up to be married in their turn. At the same time, two other priests were performing baptisms in different parts of the church. I also visited the much smaller Sioni Cathedral, near to the river, originally built about AD 600 but mainly rebuilt in the thirteenth century. I then crossed the very modern pedestrian Peace Bridge and walked back across a large new garden still being built and up the steep hill to the hotel.

Kashveti Church of St George,   *Tbilisi, with wedding in progress.*   *Sioni cathedral, Tbilisi.*

Peace Bridge, Tbilisi.   *Bells of Metekhi church, Tbilisi.*   *Tbilisi citadel by night.*

That evening we had supper in the restaurant of the old part of the hotel, with magnificent views of the city, looking across to the citadel. I had the suspicion that our rooms in the newer building, where we were all lodged, were probably less comfortable than those in the older part, and that the rooms in the older part certainly had better views. My window just looked across to a crumbling brick wall the other side of a narrow street. However, it was clean and comfortable enough, so I should not complain. All in all, I had had a fascinating holiday in a wonderful country.

The citadel, Tbilisi.

Typical house, Tbilisi.

Bells at Jvari Church, Mtskheta.

CHAPTER 10

INLAND ILLYRIA: KOSOVO AND NORTHERN ALBANIA

Fresco in Notre Dame Church, Lipjan.

For my first trip of 2012, I travelled again with Eastern Approaches, who had given me such a successful trip to Georgia the previous year. As it was to be an early flight, I decided to spend the night in the Marriot Courtyard Hotel at Gatwick. However, I went over to the Ibis for supper since Warwick Ball, the owner of the firm, was to be there as well as Rupert, the tour manager, and a few of the other travellers. Warwick arrived very late, since he had decided to come by train from Edinburgh and his train had broken down; however, I did just meet him as well as Rupert, who proved to be a former pupil of Sherborne School.

We had a comfortable and punctual flight to Pristina and were transferred to our hotel, a couple of miles out of the town, which started on the seventh floor of a tall building. The numbering of the rooms was very peculiar, the six rooms on my floor being 1, 11, 111, 9, 99, and 999. However, the room itself was comfortable and had a balcony with views to both a car scrap yard and snow-covered mountains. There was also in our rooms a list of hotel rules such as I had found in my first hotel in Albania. The most startling of these rules read, "Hazardous goods like gas cylinders, cooking stoves, inflammable fuels, firearms; etc in the hotels by guests is strictly prohibited."

Views from Pristina hotel.

We drove into the town for a leg stretch. Most of the centre had been destroyed in the Yugoslav civil war and been replaced by ugly modern concrete structures. However, there was a pleasant pedestrian precinct where we discovered a statue of Mother Teresa of Calcutta, the first of many we were to see during our trip, as well as a good bookshop and some coffee shops.

The evening meal was excellent. During the course of it, we were told that our itinerary might have to be changed since one of the mountain villages we were supposed to be visiting was snowbound. We were also told that our next hotel, at Prizren, had been changed since the original could not guarantee our booking, even if the full cost was paid in advance in cash. Back in my room, I found the bathroom light worked by movement below, and if you stood still for more than a short time, it went out, and you had to move again to get it to work.

The next morning was cloudless with a lovely temperature, and even though cloud built up later, it remained dry all day. We were first driven to the Roman remains at Upliana. On the way, we drove through the Serbian enclave of Gracanica, where many of the cars still had their old Serbian number plates and, as a result, were not allowed to be driven out of the very small area of the town into Kosovo proper. There was little left of Upliana, which was once a thriving Roman city due to its vicinity to gold mines and to a major crossroad. By chance, while we were there, the chief archaeologist of the area came by and told us a lot more about its history in classical times.

Next, we were driven back through Pristina to the site of the Battle of Kosovo of 1389, which the Serbs consider the most important date in their history, even though it was the defeat which led to their being ruled for some five hundred years by the Ottoman Turks. The area was now marked by a tall tower and some odd modern sculptures.

Upliana Roman city, near Pristina.

Site of Battle of Kosovo.

We then visited the Carshi Mosque, Pristina's oldest. It was under reconstruction, but we did manage, after clambering over duckboards, to enter the building, which was very simple but impressive.

After lunch, we walked to the Fati Mosque, which was also impressive, especially its interior paintings, before walking back to the coach via the market; we also saw a Serbian Orthodox church, started in the 1980s before the civil war but not touched since, and the university library, a modern building, with a most peculiar Eden type-domed roof.

Carshi Mosque, Pristina.

Fati Mosque, Pristina.

Uncompleted Orthodox church.

The next day started with clear blue skies, suggesting the weather forecast of "fine with increasing temperatures" would be correct. The first stop on the way to our next stay at Prizren was at the Serbian Gracanica Monastery. The walls surrounding the church were topped by barbed wire, and there was a warning sign at the entrance forbidding, among other things, the use of hand guns. However, once inside the grounds, all appeared normal; the building had mercifully not been damaged during the civil war, and a nun gave us an excellent introduction, in fine English, to the magnificent frescos.

Gracanica Monastery with entrance signs and frescos.

When we emerged from the church, we found that there had been a big change in the weather, to a bitter wind and heavy clouds threatening rain. The nearby mountains could no longer be seen due to the rain, or snow, that was falling over them.

We stopped to see the tiny basilica-type medieval church of Notre Dame in the village of Lipjan. There were the very scanty remains of external frescos, which gave no idea of the wonderful frescos on the inside. Both the church and the frescos were said to be older than Gracanica. The building was empty; services evidently now take place in a larger modern, but dull, church, which had been built next door. I can only assume that the congregation had outgrown the original church.

Church of Notre Dame, Lipjan.   *Frescos in Notre Dame, Lipjan.*

We then drove through light rain to Gadime, where we stopped for coffee by an entrance to a cave complex, only discovered in 1976. Most of us took the tour round the caves, and I was glad to do so, for they were very fine and unspoilt, except for lighting and a concrete floor, since they had never been occupied by humans. The guide demonstrated that it was possible to play a tune by striking the stalactites with his hand, producing a different note from each. Once again the weather had changed, and we emerged into bright sunlight; the weather was to remain good for the rest of the holiday.

Our picnic lunch was taken in the garden of a café with fine views of the snowy mountains in bright sunlight. The café sold a very good beer at the cost of only one euro for a fifty-millilitre bottle.

The afternoon drive was up over the pass through the Sharr Mountains National Park, and we had a short stop by the hotel where we were originally going to stay. It was a lovely journey, but none of us thought the hotel looked good, despite its fine position, so we did not regret the change.

Gadime caves.   *Sharr Mountains.*

We drove through Prizren to reach our hotel, which stood a little way out of town. I was glad to see, as we drove through, that at first glance it looked as though not too much damage had been caused in the civil war. Our hotel was new and had the surprising name of OK. It was a small hotel of just twenty rooms and nearly lived up to its name. Once again, the room numbering was weird. My room, numbered 120, was on the third floor, according to the lift, despite the number IV on the key tab. My shower was not working, but luckily room service was good, and it was soon mended. Above my basin was a little notice reading "For 2 minutes you will warm water". The lighting was poor, especially on the landing, and there was no shaver point. But the room was clean, and I had a good view from my balcony across the plain to the snow-covered mountains. We had an excellent dinner of fish taken from the hotel's own pool.

The OK Hotel, Prizren.

The following day was spent in Prizren. I found that much had changed since my previous visit nearly thirty years before. We had then been in the town on market day, and the villagers had come down from the mountains, all dressed in their own village costumes, with their donkeys and carts Now the streets were clogged with cars, mainly old, and the dress was Western, though some children's clothing shops appeared to stock just the traditional forms of clothing (though I did not see any children wearing them). Many of the old streets had not altered much, and I thought I recognised the gate through which Jacynth had been dragged on our previous visit to become an honoured guest at a wedding party (for women only, since I, with several other men, had been left outside).

Prizren shops,

Our first visit was to see the exterior of the Byzantine Church of Our Lady of Ljevis. This was protected by armed police and a barbed wire barrier on the exterior wall. We had been told that we would only be able to see the exterior since it was under restoration, but while we were looking at the exterior, arrangements were made for us to see inside before we left the next morning. That visit proved to be most interesting. It was a completely dark interior, and the frescos, also being restored, could only just be made out through the gloom. However, we were allowed to use flash photography, and these showed some fine but badly damaged frescos which had been chipped to allow plaster to be put over them during the Ottoman occupation. When we left, a woman in national dress proceeded to tell us at great length how much better things were now than before the civil war, how dreadful the Serbs had been, and how marvellous the United Nations were in driving them out (only revealing at the end that she herself lived in Chicago).

Church of Our Lady of Ljevis, Prizren, with fresco.

We then visited the archaeological museum in an old hammam. This was more interesting for the building itself than for the contents since the Serbs had taken most of the exhibits to Belgrade and had never returned them. At the Roman Catholic Cathedral, not an historic building but quite attractive, we were given a talk by a nun of St Claire, before taking coffee at an open air café and then moving on to a lovely painted building, the sixteenth-century Mosque of Sinan Pasha. This man was an Albanian Sinan and not the famous Ottoman architect of Suleyman the Magnificent. I thought it was the finest painted mosque I had yet seen (except for the one at Tetovo in the former Yugoslav Republic of Macedonia).

Prizren with Mosque of Sinan Pasha.   *Paintings in Mosque of Sinan Pasha.*

We had lunch in a Turkish restaurant before being taken to see a small factory manufacturing hand-made silver filigree. Before the civil war, there had been a silver filigree school with more than a hundred and thirty pupils. However, this then closed down, but after the war, some of those pupils got together and started a new factory. They were hoping to start a new school in the near future. Their work was of very high quality, and a lot of it was done as commission work for churches. Their work was made of 97 percent pure silver and 3 percent copper, which gave it the necessary strength.

Silver filigree workers.

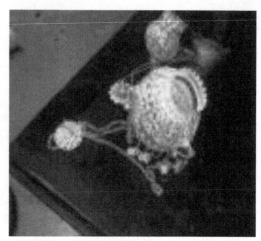

Silver filigree examples.

After a siesta back at the hotel, we were again taken into Prizren. Here, half the party decided to go shopping before supper. The rest of us started walking up the very steep path towards the citadel, from where we were told there was an excellent view of the town. About halfway up, there was a firmly locked small church and some ruined houses damaged during the civil war. Since there was also a very good view from there, two of us decided to stop at this point; we found out later that we had not really missed anything, since the citadel now consisted only of the walls and the view. Down on the level again, a group of young men persuaded me to join them and have a talk about the UK. I was not even allowed to pay for the beer they gave me.

Prizren. River and bridge.

Young men in Prizren.

Supper that evening was at a local restaurant by the river. The wine was pleasant, though I had strong doubts about the veracity of the label, which claimed it was a merlot dated 1993!

The next day, we left for Gjakove after visiting the interior of the church and the newly reconstructed building of the League of Prizren, which had been dynamited by the Serbian military police in 1999 and later rebuilt as nearly as possible to the plans of the original; we learnt a lot about the history of the town. It had been nearly the only building in the centre to have suffered. We also saw a hammam and a small Tekke.

At Gjakove, we stayed at the traditional Quarshia e Jupave Hotel, where my room had no view at all. Otherwise, it was a clean and pleasant hotel; the plumbing worked, the food was good, and there was a razor point in my room. Gjakove was unlike Prizren in that most of the bazaar area, where our hotel was located, had been destroyed in the fighting; indeed, it was possibly the worst damaged town in the whole of Kosovo but had now been reconstructed to as near as possible to what it had been before; it looked very genuine. In this way, it reminded me of Warsaw, which also was reconstructed to look as it had been before the Second World War.

Luckily, one of the buildings which was badly damaged in the fighting had been repaired. It was the elaborately painted sixteenth-century Hadim Mosque. This building even outdid the mosque in Tetovo, especially inside. It had been beautifully restored, and the remarkable paintings were supposed to be exact copies of the originals.

We were very lucky when we visited, for the delightful imam was there, accompanied by his very shy four-year-old son, Oman. He proceeded to give us a very full and interesting introduction to the mosque, well translated by our Albanian guide, Dorian (who, incidentally, accompanied us for the whole of the tour). This mosque was apparently of the Bektashi sect, which was more liberal than the Sunni and was inclined to treat women as equal to men. However, when the imam joined us for supper at the reconstructed Han the next day, he had to share a separate little table with Rupert and Dorian, for he was not allowed to sit at a table where anyone was drinking alcohol (even though he was quite happy to sit in the same room separated by only a few feet).

The Hadim Mosque, Gjakove.

The next day was hot, sunny, and busy for our full day's outing, before returning to our hotel. We first drove towards some very high mountains, topped with snow. This was the view that must have encountered the Serbian army when they had to retreat across these mountains into Albania and then to the Adriatic in the First World War. Even in the late spring, the mountains looked forbidding, and I found myself wondering what it had seemed like to those soldiers in the worst winter for many years at a time when there were no roads at all and very few tracks, so that they would have had to travel on foot through deep snow with little, if any, food.

When we reached the foot of the mountains, we made a right turn and drove past several graveyards holding both Muslim and Christian tombs and then went through what looked like the largest, and most decrepit, second-hand car market in the world. We continued on through Decani and Pec to a track leading to the source of the White River, over a kilometre away, along which we had to walk. It was worth the walk, however, to see how the river emerged from the rock cliffs in a series of waterfalls.

Track to the White River.   *A White River waterfall.*

We next drove through Pec to see the magnificent Patriarchate Church. Pec itself had changed out of recognition since the civil war. On my last visit, the town had been filled with narrow streets and houses built of grey stone, many of them tower houses, with very few windows looking out onto the street. A very enclosed community. During the fighting, most of these houses had been destroyed and were now replaced by modern apartment blocks.

The church itself was a little way out of the town, up towards the mountains at the foot of the Rugovo Gorge. Luckily, this church had not been much affected by the fighting, though many changes had taken place. The first noticeable change was that the extensive outer walls (it had once been a fortified church) were now crowned by barbed wire, and there was a small military encampment of United Nations troops just outside, together with a number of military vehicles, for it was protected round the clock to make sure it was not damaged, as were so many of the smaller Serbian Orthodox churches during the fighting. Kosovo was now mainly Albanian and Muslim, and there was still a great deal of bitterness between the Serbs and Albanians; this was still very much a Serb church, and there was a great fear that damage might be done to it were this protection to be withdrawn. Kosovo was still considered by the Serbs to be part of their inheritance, and they have not recognised Kosovo as a separate country.

We were kept waiting for quite a time by the military, presumably while they checked our credentials, before we were eventually allowed to drive up to the entrance gate and disembark. I had remembered the church itself as having been built of grey stone, and several of my travel books show this to have been the case, but the exterior was now plastered and painted a deep red.

The Patriarchate Church of Pec.

This church was noted for its frescos, many of them dating from the mid-fourteenth century. There were three churches here, all united under one roof by an atrium. Our excellent guide, a nun, took us around and explained most of the magnificent frescos to us.

Frescos in Pec Patriarchate Church.

We were all rather amused at one point when she had to scrabble in her habit to find her mobile phone to take a call, and then while she was still speaking to her caller, she had to do the same again to take another call on a second mobile.

We were allowed a good time to look around before being taken back to the coach to be driven up to the top of the Rugovo Gorge; the monastery was at the entrance to the gorge. Before the civil war, I had driven a car a few miles up the gorge before deciding that enough was enough. Once again, I marvelled at the fact that the retreating Serbian army had managed to make its way up this route in the winter of 1915/1916. I could not understand why the authorities allowed coaches to use the road, for there were a couple of occasions when our guide had to dismount to direct the driver round corners, with only inches from the edge of a precipitous drop to the river below; at the same time, there was an overhanging rock with an equally small clearance for the roof of the coach. When we eventually reached the opening of the gorge at the top, there was a restaurant with a very difficult turn into it but which gave us a good trout lunch with freshly caught fish.

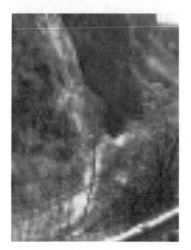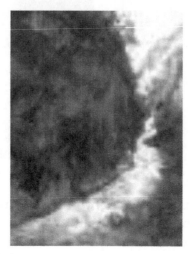

Rugovo Gorge, with river and snowdrift.

We then took the perilous journey down and were once again stopped by the military when we reached their watch tower near the Patriarchate before finally being allowed to continue on our way to the monastery at Decani.

UN military post, Pec.

As with the church at Pec, the monastery at Decani was situated a little way out of the town towards the mountains, and as at Pec, it too was guarded by United Nations troops; once again, we were delayed before being allowed through.

The church itself was made from a two-coloured marble that looked almost white in the bright sunlight; it differed from the other Serbian churches that I had seen in the number of external carvings of animals and people. Inside it was very dark, since a lot of restoration work was in progress, though we were able to see the magnificent frescos through the gloom, including the wonderful fresco of the Stem of Jesse, which had remained vividly in my memory from earlier visits so many years before. As this was a monastery, our guide was a monk. The number of monks living at the monastery was apparently now increasing, but he would not discuss how the present relationship with the Kosovan inhabitants in Decani was progressing. One can only hope that the need for this military protection of the churches will soon prove to be unnecessary; with time, the fact that they were Serbian in origin could cease to be of significance and they will be recognised for what they are: magnificent buildings from a previous age. Catholic churches did not have to be protected in the same way, so it was not a religious matter (despite the fact that the vast majority of the inhabitants of Kosovo were now Albanian Muslims). It was still the hatred of the Serbs, and the memory of the war in which so many Serbian churches and Muslim mosques were destroyed, that caused trouble.

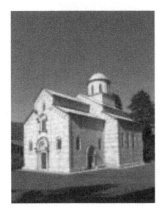  

Decani church with carvings and part of Stem of Jesse fresco.

Upon our return to Gjakove, we had more time to explore the reconstructed bazaar before having a good meal at the Han, where we were also entertained by some local musicians.

The next day, a Sunday, we were woken by the sound of church bells from a nearby Catholic church, not a sound we had expected to hear in a Muslim area. After breakfast, we left to cross the frontier to Albania. On the outskirts of the town, we stopped to see a many-arched Ottoman bridge, one of the best I had seen since the bridge at Arta in Greece.

Ottoman bridge near Gjakove.

The road to and across the frontier ran through attractive hilly country, with snow-topped mountains not far away on our right.

Country near the Albanian-Kosovan frontier.

At the frontier, all our passports had to be inspected and stamped, but since they were taken in a pile and we did not have to be seen individually, the stop was brief. We soon reached Bayram Curri,.where our hotel for the next night was situated, but as our rooms were not yet ready, we only stopped for coffee before transferring into two minibuses for our trip. It took well over an hour to drive twenty-five kilometres, up the Valbona Valley to a lovely restaurant in the middle of the "Accursed Mountains", as one travel book called them. The road was certainly "Accursed", though the scenery was magnificent and our coach would certainly never have made the ascent. We ate the meat of our excellent lunch with our fingers, as local custom dictated, and we next paid a visit to an attractive mountain village nearby, which the inhabitants were hoping to turn into a ski resort.

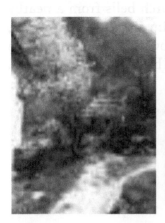

Village in the Albanian "Accursed Mountains".

We then sat down at a table in the open air to be given Raki and Turkish coffee, before returning once again to Bayram Curri, where we were given the choice of going to our hotel or visiting a tower house. Since I had visited tower houses on several occasions, I opted to return to the hotel. This proved to be very basic, and the stairs were exceedingly dangerous, with no banisters and large drops, though I was lucky enough to have a clean room, which was more than several of the party experienced. When it came to supper, the meat was uneatable. The manager told Dorian, "If you come again and the food is as bad, we will refund all your money." All in all, it was far and away the worst hotel of our trip, but there was no other hotel in the town.

The next morning, we had to leave at 5.30 a.m. in order to catch the Lake Komana passenger ferry, which was due to leave at 6.15. We had originally been scheduled to catch a vehicular ferry at 7.00, but the government had withdrawn its subsidy so it had ceased to function a few weeks previously. The last three kilometres of the journey was up a track off the proper road, and this proved to be under reconstruction. Our coach just managed with inches to spare to squeeze in between the parked road works vehicles, but a few hundred yards further on, it was quite unable to negotiate a sharp, narrow corner in the mud, and we all had to start walking. Dorian spoke on his mobile phone and arranged for the ferry to wait for us and then, somehow, managed to rustle up a rusty old minibus, which managed to catch us up and, in two separate journeys, carry us the rest of the way. Boarding the ferry was very difficult because of the piles of mud and rusty metal over which we had to clamber to reach the exceedingly narrow, bouncy gangplank (with no side railings at all). I do not know how we all managed it without anyone falling off. The ferry itself was very ancient and rusty; indeed, there was one point on the walkway around outside the cabin where the floor had developed a hole through which we could see the water below.

Boarding the Lake Komana ferry.

The cabin itself seated about twenty people, and with our group, most of the seats were taken. We finally left only twenty-five minutes late. The lake itself was rather like a fjord and was one of several joined together by a dam and a hydroelectric scheme, which we were to reach some two and a half hours later. The scenery was lovely with cliffs and mountains, many of them snow topped, rising on either side.

What we had not expected was the number of stops we made to take on further passengers; we ended up with about sixty in all, a number which was grossly excessive for the size and seaworthiness of the boat. At none of the stops was there a proper quay, and the passengers were often waiting in the mud, without any visible foot access. An elderly lady and her husband had arrived at one of these stops carried on a donkey, and a small boy had come with them to take the donkey home. At another of these places, the captain misjudged where he was going, and the boat made alarming sounds as it scraped along the bottom. A second attempt to reach the land was no more successful, and only on the third attempt did we reach a position from where the gangplank could be pushed out to reach those intending to board. Once we were on our way again, the captain gave some orders to the solitary crew member, who came out to the walkway, lifted a metal hatch, and descended into the hold, presumably to make sure that the boat was not letting in water through any damage done by the scraping. All appeared to be sound, though the crew member lifted the hatch and peered in several times during the course of the journey. Eventually, a few buildings and a stone quay heralded the end of our journey, and we fought our way off against the large crowd trying to board for the return journey. Some of our fellow passengers crowded onto small boats to take them to their destinations, and others boarded vehicles waiting for them.

Lake Komana picking-up point.

Some passengers on their next transport.

We found two minibuses waiting for us, which took us through a long very low tunnel, which was the only land exit from the quayside. Our coach would never have been able to drive through it; indeed, our minibuses were the largest vehicles which could have fitted below the roof. We were told the tunnel had been built for the hydroelectric station when it was erected, though how any of the heavy machinery could have been carried to the site was never explained.

There followed a drive through some lovely country and a coffee stop overlooking a large lake; we reached the main road again, where we found our coach waiting for us. We then stopped at a wayside restaurant for a good lunch before reaching the city of Shkodra in mid-afternoon. The hotel proved to the best one we had stayed in during the whole of our tour, indeed it was better than any hotel I had stayed in at all in Albania. I was particularly lucky in that I was given a luxurious large room in the front of the hotel with a large balcony, carrying the flags of many nations, overlooking a large new mosque. The only disadvantages were that the bathroom fittings were all of a very modern design, so that my universal plug would not fit in the basin, and that the call to prayer at about four in the morning was a particularly loud one and woke me each night of our stay. Some of the others in the group had rooms overlooking a church, and they were equally disturbed by the noise of the church bells ringing, though not at quite such an unearthly hour.

The hotel at Shkodra.

Bathroom in the hotel.

That evening, we were taken to dine at a restaurant a few miles out of Shkodra, right near the Montenegrin frontier. When we reached the coach, we found that one elderly member of our party was missing. We were kept waiting for some time while her room was checked and a general search was made for her before eventually leaving without her or Rupert, who was left to try and find her. She was eventually discovered having gone out for a walk, despite the fact that we had been clearly told what time we were to meet, and Rupert had to bring her out by taxi to join us.

The next day, we were due to drive into the Albanian Alps to see a village called Theti, often rated the most beautiful village in Albania. Unfortunately, it was still snowbound, so while some of us were taken to see Kruja, where the castle had been turned into a museum for Skanderbeg (the national hero of Albania), six of the party who had visited Kruja before were taken off by Dorian to cross the Montenegrin border to see Kotor. I had visited Kruja during my tour of Albania (see chapter 1), but I had also visited Kotor on four or five previous occasions, and since the Kruja tour would also visit Lezhe, the original burial place of Skanderbeg, where I had not been, I went with the main group. While we were on the way, Dorian phoned through to say they had not been able to cross the frontier into Montenegro, since at the crossing, the frontier police had discovered that his international driving license had expired just two days earlier, so the party was just going to an Adriatic beach (he had not thought to check it, since he had not envisaged doing any driving outside Albania).

Lezhe was where Skanderbeg had originally been buried, though his bones had later been dug up by the Ottomans, who had taken them off wrapped in gold or silver as treasure. However, his original tomb was still preserved, in its original simple building, under a modern protective concrete covering, in a small park, overlooked by a church standing on the edge of a cliff.

Skanderbeg's tomb, Lezhe.   Church at Lezhe.

Kruja was far more "touristified" than it had been on my previous visit, and the shops on the bazaar street sold much more in the way of tourist tat; the nearby roads now also had many stalls on them. At the Skanderbeg Museum, we were given a very good guide to show us round, but he could not rouse any enthusiasm in me, apart from the magnificent entrance.

However, after lunch in an open air café in the castle grounds, four of us visited a lovely little Tekke a bit below where the keeper, who knew not a word of English, still managed to explain everything clearly and showed us the tombs of the holy people as well as the room where the Dervishes used to dance. He also explained that in the Bektashi sect, both men and women were considered equal in every way.

Entrance to museum, Kruja.   Tekke, Kruja.   Skanderbeg statue, Kruja.

Our final day was to be spent in Shkodra itself. It was interesting to see, when walking round the city, that even though Albania was a Muslim country, very few of the women wore head coverings of any sort. Indeed, there were no dress laws such as they had in Iran.

Our first visit was to the photographic museum, which had a wonderful record of the history of northern Albania and Shkodra from 1838, when Marubi, a political refugee, took the first photograph ever taken in the country. There were some 150,000 photographs taken by him and his adopted son from that time up till the reign of King Zog. Only a few of these were able to be displayed in the small and rather run-down building, but plans were afoot for a new and much larger building to be made available, where many more of this fine historical record can be shown. Our next visit was to the Historic and Archaeological Museum in an attractive old house with some good exhibits. After coffee in a café in the grounds of what used to be the British Consulate, we drove out to see a remarkably fine, many-arched Ottoman bridge, even better than the one near Gjakove.

Shkodra Museum.   *Ottoman bridge, Shkodra.*   *Shkodra Museum.*

After lunch, which we took in an open air café overlooking the large lake, part of which was in Montenegro, we were given free time, much of which I occupied in walking round the city. I saw a mixture of old and modern buildings, for Enver Hoxha had pulled down much of the old to build new factories. Luckily, most of these were out of the main town, for they were now mainly derelict and crumbling into ruin. One of the buildings I wanted to see more closely was a new painted mosque, which we had driven past several times. I was also pleased to find that one of the main streets was called Edith Durham; she was a great British expert on Albania at the start of the twentieth century and wrote several books about her journeys through this still little-known land; she was still considered almost as a saint by the Albanians. I also found several more statues of Mother Teresa.

Street sign, Shkodra.   *Mother Teresa statue.*   *New mosque, Shkodra.*

We assembled in the evening to be taken up to the castle, which stood on a very high hill above Shkodra, to see the fine all-round view of the sunset, before visiting a typical Albanian restaurant with music and some dancing as well as very fine Lebanese-style food for our final evening meal.

Sunset from citadel, Shkodra.   *Albanian restaurant, Shkodra.*

The next morning, our departure for the airport was not without incident. Our coach driver parked as near to the hotel as possible to make it easier to load our cases. A traffic warden objected and ordered the coach to be moved. When this had been done, he called the police, who had to pass the whole episode to the city council, who then had to pass it to the mayor, who told them all not to be so stupid and said we must be allowed to go at once. Although we left an hour late, we still had time to stop for coffee at a seaside restaurant. A part of the building next door was collapsed on the beach, not because of bad construction but because it had been pulled down for being built without planning permission. The rest of our journey was uneventful.

Punishment for building without planning permission.

CHAPTER 11

ARMENIA AND NAGORNO KARABAGH

Haghartsin Monastery.

The second trip I was to make in 2012 had one similarity with the first, in that Nagorno Karabagh was, like Kosovo, a self-declared republic. However, unlike Kosovo, no other country in the world had formally recognised it (although Armenia gave it a lot of support). Well over 90 percent of the population was of Armenian origin, and the language was Armenian, as was the currency. The religion also was of the Armenian Apostolic Church. However, despite the fact that the war between Armenia and Azerbaijan ended in a cease-fire in 1994, when the Armenians had gained superiority, the inhabitants desired to become free of Azerbaijan, regardless of the fact that it was well within the frontiers of that country. Nagorno Karabagh determined to rule itself. Its only physical connection with the outer world was a strip of land fifty kilometres wide, with one main road joining it to Armenia. Otherwise, it was totally surrounded by Azerbaijan. My journey was a tailor-made trip by myself in a car driven by my guide.

There was chaos at the departure from Heathrow. The plane was due to fly on to Iran from Yerevan, and there was a large body of Iranians who had come from the United States, wishing to bring all their luggage as hand luggage, regardless as to how large or heavy it was or how many pieces there were. Several of them would not accept the fact that they would only be allowed one piece of hand luggage each and that the rest would have to be put in the hold; they hurled abuse at the desk staff, who behaved with remarkable politeness and dignity, and eventually we were able to board, though the Iranians were still not happy.

However, we had a good flight despite the fact that the captain gave us the wrong Yerevan time when we were landing. He must have thought that Iran was in the same time zone as Armenia, though there is an hour's difference.

I had a tedious time on landing, for after queuing for some time to obtain a visa, I was then told to go and change money so that I could pay for it in the Armenian currency. When this formality was completed, there was a queue at the passport desk before going to obtain the luggage. Even then, matters were not quite finished, for I was not allowed to leave with my luggage until I could show the luggage number given at the check-out at Heathrow. I had never been asked for this before but fortunately knew just where the piece of paper was.

Luckily, George, my guide/driver, was still waiting for me and had soon driven me in his vehicle (smaller than a minibus but definitely a car of sorts, while looking rather like a van) to my hotel, the Aviatrans, which proved to be in a very convenient position near Republic Square. To my surprise, I was in a suite, the first room of which had a sofa, table, chair, desk, and minibar. Then there was a small lobby with a bathroom off it with an excellent bath and shower. The bedroom, opposite the bathroom, was large and comfortable, with two twin-size beds in it. I slept like a log.

Breakfast the next morning was a buffet-type meal with plenty of choice of good food, such that it would not have been a deprivation to miss out on lunch (not that George ever allowed me to miss either lunch or supper). The weather on this first day was hot, with the temperature rising up to 34 degrees Celsius, and sunny. Our first visit was to the military cemetery up on a hill, with what would have been fine views over to Mount Ararat had it not been for the heat haze, which rendered it almost invisible. Many of the tombstones were flat on the ground, like those I had found in Albania, but others stood upright and were of the Russian style, with faces of the dead on them. There was also a small church shaped like a bullet. The whole was in a beautifully kept garden.

Military cemetery, Yerevan.

We carried on to visit the Parajanov Museum. Parajanov was a film producer. His film *The Colour of Pomegranates* was described by the *Times* as the most beautiful film ever made. It was certainly a remarkable film, and Jacynth and I saw it on three different occasions, a record for us. The museum, which was in his own house, showed him to have been a very peculiar man; it was one of the most remarkable small museums I had ever visited. Apart from being a film producer, he was an artist, and the museum showed many of his works (some of them, to my mind, were hideous and others lovely, but they were all unusual). It also showed his bedroom and a living room, as well as some photographs of the prison where he was kept for some time, and then of several leaders in the USSR, on occasions when he was in favour with the authorities.

Next we went to what was called the Cascade. This was situated on a tall slope and was to display a series of waterfalls with rooms and museums, hidden by the water, behind them. But no water ran, for the project was never completed because of the disastrous earthquake of 1988. However, work had recently restarted, and there was an attractive museum of glass objects on the bottom layer and an internal lift which travelled right up to the top, so that the Cascade may soon be completed. At the bottom, there was a small park which displayed a number of statues, including three works by the well-known British artist Lynn Chadwick and two by the Welsh artist Barry Flanagan. The most amusing of the sculptures was the one of a very fat cat, which was installed to mark the reopening of the escalator.

Parajanov Museum, Yerevan.   *Lynn Chadwick sculpture at the Cascade Yerevan and the Fat Cat.*

There were many sculptures all around the city, including, in one of the main streets, one of an old flower seller. This man was an alcoholic but a rather loveable character who used to stand in the street to sell flowers until he had gathered enough money for his next bout of drinking, at which stage he would give away the rest of his flowers to any children who were nearby. So it was not only the important who are recognised in this way. I was also taken to see another huge statue, called Mother Armenia, who was holding a sword which was seventy-four metres high from the base (the figure itself being twenty-seven metres high), inside which there was a small museum to the Nagorno Karabagh war against Azerbaijan.

Old Flower Seller, Yerevan.   *Mother Armenia, Yerevan.*

We had lunch in an open air café at the bottom of the Cascade, where I discovered that the amount of money George had been given for my meals allowed for a drink of beer at lunch and a glass of wine at the evening meal. This was a welcomed surprise, for I had been expecting to pay for all my drinks (my itinerary gave me full board outside Yerevan and half board in the city itself).

After lunch, we visited a neighbouring museum (where George's mother worked), which held Russian pictures donated by an Armenian doctor who had worked in Russia. He obviously had a very good eye, for there were some excellent pictures.

We also visited the Matenaderan, which was built in 1957 to house some 15,000 Armenian manuscripts. This building had proved not nearly large enough, and a larger building had been attached to the old. All the exhibits were now in the new building, while the old was being restored so that eventually a much larger part of the collection could be displayed. Even now, it was a remarkable display. Items included the oldest printed Armenian book, printed in Venice in 1512 (though no printing press appeared in Armenia itself until about 1770). The largest book in the world, weighing twenty-four kilograms and made from the skins of sixty small cats used for parchment, was displayed in the same case as the smallest book, the size of a thumbnail.

One of my other memories of the day was of sentries from a British Guards Regiment standing on guard outside the British Embassy; they were dressed in their full red uniform, including bearskins, all this in a temperature of well over 30 degrees Celsius.

I took supper in the evening in an underground restaurant, which I thought George had suggested. I then discovered that George's recommendation was nearby, also underground, and through an even more hidden entrance, so I went there the next evening; I found the food pleasant but not quite as good and the whole place too touristified for my taste. Back in Yerevan after the tour, I once again went to the place I had discovered and recommended it to George for future use.

After supper, I returned to my hotel and found crowds gathering in Republic Square for the nightly show of light, music, and fountains. This show exceeded all expectations, with the fountains changing colour and shape according to the music that was being played. The music itself varied from classical to modern.

Light, music, and fountain show, Republic Square, Yerevan.

The next day, we were to have a long morning outside the city. The weather proved to be sunny and even hotter, reaching 36 degrees Celsius. Our first visit was to the much-restored Roman temple of Garni. This was claimed to be the farthest east Roman temple in existence. It was high above a deep valley with lovely views. It stood until 1679, when it fell in an earthquake; its foundations had been much weakened over the years by the inhabitants digging holes into the lower part of the building, looking for treasure (the holes could still be seen). The rebuilding in the 1960s and 1970s was well done. When we were there, some lovely flute music was being played in the temple itself. Nearby, there was also the excavation of a fine Roman bath house. George was able to obtain a key for the building so that I could inspect the interior; its mosaic floor was still in position.

Roman temple at Garni, near Yerevan. View from Garni.

We then moved on to the remarkable cave monastery of Gerhard. This place was one of the great religious centres in Armenia, and since it was within such an easy distance of Yerevan, it was almost always full of visitors. It was very different from any other church I had seen in Armenia, since only part of it was built out of stone and the rest was carved out of, and into, the rock cliff. It was also the place where the spear that pierced the side of Jesus at the time of the crucifixion was supposed to have rested (though the relic had now been moved to the treasury at Ejmiatsin). Inside, the church was very dark, though hundreds of candles had been lit in different places by the pilgrims, and they, as well as the few openings to the outside, gave enough light to see the remarkable carvings on the rock walls. Carvings were a feature of many Armenian churches, but Geghard was different in that its carvings were inside rather than on the outer walls. While we were there, we saw a man on the roof outside of the church cleaning the domes and their drums. I was also interested to see that a tree in the premises was still covered with rags, which pilgrims placed as some sort of prayer.

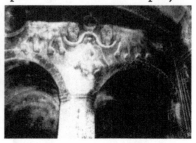

Geghard monastery, near Yerevan,

We returned to Yerevan for a late lunch in an open air restaurant in an attractive park before going to see the Genocide Memorial and Museum. This horrific event was remembered in memorials in every Armenian church I visited, and there was even a small museum in the grounds of the Armenian church in Isfahan in Iran. This main museum was subterranean, running under part of the memorial, and had a large number of exhibits, labelled in several languages, including English. I was particularly interested in the photographs of Van in Turkey both before and immediately after the genocide. It was reckoned that well over one million Armenians were killed by the Turks in 1915. A letter sent by the American consul of the time read, "I do not believe there has ever been a massacre in the history of the world so general and thorough as that which is now being perpetuated in this region, or that a more fiendish, diabolical scheme has ever been conceived in the mind of man." Hitler obviously learnt from this when he said, "Who remembers the Armenians now?" when he was embarking on the Holocaust.

Genocide Memorial, Yerevan.

That evening, after supper in George's recommended restaurant, I emerged just as a procession was starting to march to Republic Square. There were several bands, soldiers, men in wheelchairs, and hundreds of men, women, and children; they all (with the exception of the soldiers and an excellent female band, who wore their own special uniforms) dressed in the colours of the Armenian national flag. This proved to be the National Flag Day, the first one ever celebrated. Luckily, I had my reserve camera with me so that I was able to capture the celebrations, for it was a remarkably colourful occasion.

Flag Day ceremony, Yerevan.

The next day, we were to travel to a town called Goris, which was the nearest town to the frontier to Nagorno Karabagh. Once again, it was a lovely sunny day, though unfortunately there was cloud concealing the top of Mount Ararat. Our first stop was to be at Khor Virap Monastery, which was right near to the foothills of that mountain; in the right conditions, there was a marvellous view. On the road, we discovered a woman had laid a carpet right over half the road and was busy washing and scrubbing it, regardless of the traffic. Khor Virap itself was situated on a hill and could be seen over the plain from a considerable distance. It was an attractive building, though not as remarkable as some of the other Armenian churches. In one of the buildings, there was still the deep hole in which Gregory the Illuminator, the maker of the Armenian alphabet, was held as prisoner for thirteen years (he was released in 301 after performing a miracle for the king and became the founder of Christianity in the country).

Khor Virap Monastery, below Mount Ararat.

We then drove on to Noravank Monastery. I had forgotten the deep gorge we entered and then the drive steadily uphill until we finally reached our destination. When Jacynth and I had visited it many years before, both the churches had been under scaffolding, and the whole place was deserted except for the workmen, who had insisted that we join them for their picnic lunch, which consisted mainly of salad, cold meat, and many different types of bottles, all of which proved to have the same contents: vodka. Now there were a number of cars and vans as well as three coaches. The restorations were long finished, and it was obviously a popular place for a weekend visit. The first main building was a striking two-storey construction, the lower part of which was a mausoleum and the upper part a church. There were clearly no health and safety laws, for the church was reached by a very narrow and steep pair of external staircases, with a steep drop on the outside and no railings. On my previous visit, the scaffolding had acted as a railing, and even then it had not been easy. Now only the young and foolhardy attempted the climb. I dread to think how many accidents there have been over the years.

Noravank Monastery.

Both buildings sported external carvings of great skill, which showed a decidedly Eastern origin; one of them was most unusual, showing a representation of God himself holding up his right hand in blessing while holding a head in his other hand. This was probably meant to be the head of John the Baptist, since the church was dedicated to him. There were also many khachkars in the grounds, wonderfully carved tombstones of which there are many thousands in the country; it was said that no two were exactly the same as each other.

Carving of Mary and Jesus and carving of God, Noravank. *Khachkars, Noravank.*

After lunch in the new café, we drove back to the main road and up into the high mountains over a pass 2,350 metres high. There was a notable drop in temperature, from 32 degrees at Khor Virap to 23 at the head of the pass. At one point, we drove along by the frontier with Iran and near to a crossing point. All along the road here, there were a large number of stalls, all advertising Coca Cola. This particular area of Armenia, known as Areni, was famous as producing the finest red wine in the country. We stopped at one of these stalls, where we were given several wines to try. When we had chosen one, the wine was poured into a large Coca Cola bottle. This was how those crossing into Iran were able to take wine into that country, where alcohol was strictly forbidden. There was a small party of French at our hotel in Goris who could not understand why a waitress came to our table carrying a tray with two wine glasses and a large bottle of Coca Cola. Their tour guide, who proved to be a colleague of George, explained to them the reasons, and we allowed a few of them a taste from our Coca Cola bottle.

On the way to Goris, we encountered several large herds of sheep all across the road, accompanied by fearsome-looking dogs and being led by goats, and the leader always seemed to have crossed horns. These, and some herds of cattle, were usually under the care of a few mounted cowboys, who looked exactly like something out of a Wild West film.

The hotel itself was small and simple but clean, and the staff were all friendly. It had not yet been completed, and the way to the dining room was down some breeze block steps, which had not yet been roofed over. There was some heavy rain that evening, and the steps became very slippery, so that great care had to be taken. Luckily, the food, as well as the wine, was good.

The next day, the weather started with cloud, mist, and drizzle. The mist and drizzle soon cleared, though it remained cloudy for most of the day. We drove first to see the cave village in Khndzoresk. This we looked at from across a deep valley. It was in a very attractive position on the other side of the gorge but was not as exciting as those I had seen the previous year in Georgia; some of the caves were still used for storage, and a number were lived in for a time during the Karabagh war by refugees from Goris, when that town was being shelled by Azerbaijan. We next drove to see the spectacular Tatev Monastery. There were two ways of reaching this. The first was by the aerial tramway, at five and a half kilometres, the longest in the world. The second, which we took, was to drive right down into the deep gorge, past the Devil's Bridge, where a huge fallen boulder crossed the stream, and near which a small bathing pool had been fashioned, and then up a very steep slope to the monastery itself.

Khndzoresk.   *Gorge and Devil's Bridge on road to Tatev Monastery.*

This monastery was in one of the most beautiful situations of any building I had seen. It sat on the top of a cliff overlooking the gorge, with fine views over the surrounding countryside. It was a Sunday when we visited, and there was a service happening in the church while we were there. Armenian services usually lasted for over three hours, and there were no pews, only a few chairs for the elderly and disabled (when Jacynth and I had attended a service in Ejmiatsin back in 1989, my only previous visit to the country, we had been firmly put in two seats as being the only foreigners present). They were similar to many Orthodox services in the way that worshippers entered and left as they wished during the service, and few attended for the whole time. I followed the local custom. There was usually a large amount of music during the service, on this occasion sung by a female choir. The priest had an assistant, a boy whose voice had not yet broken, who sang quite a large part of the ceremony solo, and who also, on one occasion, processed around the church swinging a censer giving off clouds of incense; he stopped at one point to have a chat with a woman, possibly his mother. George told me that this position was usually given to someone who was intended for the priesthood later on.

Tatev Monastery near Goris.

Apart from the Church of St Peter and St Paul, dating from about 900, there was a smaller Church of St Gregory (1295) attached to the main church and the Church of the Mother of God built over the entrance, with apparently no foundations. There were several other ancillary buildings built into the walls. In the complex, there was also the tomb of St Gregory and an obelisk known as a Gavesan, built of small stones and with a small cornice and a khachkar on top. This was built higher than the wall and used to sway; according to one legend, if an enemy approached, the monks would push it back and forth so that the potential enemy would see it moving and think that only giants would be able to do that and therefore give up their proposed attack. Another version was that it would sway as a warning if there was an earthquake. It no longer worked and had iron bands around its base to keep it stable.

Gateway to Tatev Monastery.

Tomb of St Gregory.

The Gavesan.

On our return to Goris, we had time to explore the attractive little town, which was unusual since there were none of the normal communist tower blocks; indeed, the vast majority of the buildings were only one storey. While it was situated on the sides of and in a very deep valley, it was laid out in a rectangular grid pattern. It was lucky that it was not badly damaged in the Azerbaijani bombardment during the recent war; indeed, the pleasant little eighteenth-century church was only just missed by an artillery shell.

There was a thunderstorm and heavy rain during the night, but this was over by the time we left the next morning, though we left for Nagorno Karabagh in thick fog and a light drizzle, which was a disappointment, for there should have been magnificent mountain views in the country through which we were driving. Luckily, by the time we reached the frontier post, the drizzle had stopped and the fog was disappearing; there were even some patches of blue sky. The crossing of the frontier was quick, just a showing of passports, and although the corridor from Armenia was only fifty kilometres wide, there was no sign of any military presence. At one point during the drive, we saw a wire stretched across the gorge beside us, which was apparently left over from the recent war and had been placed there to deter low-flying Azerbaijani aircraft. Our first call was to the hilltop town of Shushi, where we stopped at a nineteenth-century cathedral.

Shushi Cathedral, Nagorno Karabagh.　　*A main street in Shushi with gas pipe over road.*

At the outbreak of the war, Shushi was mainly occupied by Azeris and stood in a strong position overlooking Stepanakert, the capital city of Karabagh; for a year, the capital was bombarded. Eventually, the Armenians managed to scale a footpath up the cliff and captured the town. The scars of the war were still very evident, for many of the buildings were in ruins, and several of the main streets were no more than muddy tracks. However, there had been some regeneration recently. The cathedral itself, which had been unused for religious services during the Soviet occupation, was spared during the war, when the Azeris used it as an ammunition store, knowing that the Armenians would never shell such an important Christian building. It had been well restored, unlike some exceedingly large, very shabby blocks of Soviet flats opposite, some of which were derelict shells and others still lived in (but now by Armenians). The town mosque was deserted, though undamaged except by grass and weeds growing through the courtyard and on the roof of the building.

We lunched in a new hotel, which otherwise seemed empty, before the short drive down to Stepanakert. Unlike Shushi, all signs of the war had disappeared, and there was plenty of new building taking place. We first parked on the main street, right outside the Foreign Office, where we had been instructed to go so that I could obtain my visa. I just filled in a form, which George took into an office with my passport and came out to say everything would be completed in an hour. He then took me to the Karabagh War Museum, small but interesting with a good English-speaking guide, before taking me to our surprisingly modern and comfortable hotel, which was attached to the parliament building, in an attractive very broad street and opposite the Presidential Palace.

Hotel and parliament building, Stepanakert.

New building, possibly theatre, Stepanakert.

While George went to retrieve my passport and visa, I set out to explore the city on foot. Since there were only 35,000 inhabitants, I was able to cover quite a lot of the place. One very attractive new building, almost completed, was a little down the hill from the hotel and looked as if it was to be a theatre or opera house. Nearer to the hotel was another fine fountain which, after dark, was to give a light and music display (though smaller and less grand than that in Yerevan).

That evening, we had an excellent meal in an open air restaurant before joining in the *corsa*, the daily evening parade of many of the citizens. My first impression of this place was of a calm, friendly, and confident town, and there seemed to be no fear of war breaking out again, despite the fact that while we were there, several men of both sides were killed in frontier skirmishes. Although it used Armenian currency and the Armenian language, it was fiercely independent and had its own flag, elected parliament, and president. His palace, incidentally, was obviously a slightly older Russian-style building. I had not known what to expect of the city, but it was certainly nothing like this.

The next day started sunny and remained fine for most of the day, until there was a sudden heavy downpour while we were driving back to the hotel from our day's visits. We started by driving out of the town past a huge modern sculpture, in a red stone, which I was told was supposed to represent the grandfather and grandmother of Armenia. I had wanted to stop and take a photograph of this remarkable sculpture, but it was being cleaned at the time, and quite a large part of it was concealed by a crane. Even when I did take a picture of it the next day, the crane can still be seen in the background. Another large sculptured head in a similar stone also stood in the hotel grounds. Many sculptures can be found in

Karabagh, as indeed they can be in Armenia. One of the more conventional ones stood in front of the fountain near our hotel and depicted Stepan, the founder of the city.

Grandfather and Grandmother of Armenia, Stepanakert.   *Sculpture head in hotel grounds, Stepanakert.*

The road we took steadily deteriorated as we travelled farther from the city, though sections labelled on signs saying that the road had been built by "the whole Armenian People" had not yet deteriorated as much as the rest. We also encountered several large signs erected by the Halo Foundation, saying that the area had now been cleared of land mines (though there were never any signs to show how large the area was). Several pieces of what looked like cultivatable land had been left untended, suggesting there were still mines in those areas. At one point, we passed some large refineries, some of the metal being gold from nearby mines, after which the road became even more horrible to drive, though the mountain and river views were lovely. Eventually, we turned off the road onto a track which my guide book said was driveable by 4WD vehicles (though George managed) and eventually sighted our destination: the Dadivank Monastery. This was not at present an active place, but was under restoration. It was the supposed burial place of St Thaddeus, a first-century Christian martyr. The first church dated from the eleventh century and the cathedral from 1214. There seemed to be only one custodian, who tried to sell some religious trinkets at the entrance. I should not think he did very well, seeing the difficulty of reaching the place. While we were there, a taxi with one passenger did arrive just as we were leaving, but we saw no sign of other visitors nor other cars on the road.

Dadivank Monastery, Nagorno Karabagh.

We spent quite a long time at Dadivank, which was an interesting place. When we reached the road again, we retraced our route. George told me that if we had continued along, there was another crossing into Armenia, but that it was hardly ever used since the road was even worse farther on; the road from Goris to Shushi was really the only practical physical connection Karabagh had with the outside world.

On our return, we took on fuel at a small place near the metal refinery. George's car was adapted to take LPG, which was a lot cheaper. The only disadvantage was that a lot of the filling stations were very old. We were made to leave the car and sit some distance away while the filling took place. This operation often took as long as twenty minutes, though one modern station at which we filled up only took about five minutes.

Next, we stopped for a late lunch in a charming garden in a roadside café, which was run by a retired schoolmaster who told us how Stalin had kept people separated to stop them joining up in some nationalistic movement. There was a village only five kilometres away, but they had not been allowed to build a road there, so the only way to reach it was by a thirty-kilometre detour. He had a delightful nine-year-old son who presented me with a stone cross he had made. When we left, we were presented with a bottle of home-made wine.

From here, we drove up a steep hill to the Gandzasar Monastery, the church of which was built between 1232 and 1238 with the gavit, a burial place attached to the church, being added some twenty-five years later. There were very fine views from the church. This proved to be a very active monastery; they had almost finished building a new seminary for the training of priests and monks. The building was particularly noted for its many fine carvings. I also met two English visitors, almost the only English people I saw in the whole of my trip.

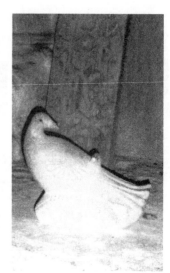

Gandzasar Monastery, Vank, Nagorno Karabagh.

The village of Vank, below the hill, was also an unusual place. To start with, there was a large wall covered with car number plates. These were apparently taken from cars originally owned by Azeris but abandoned when they fled during the war. There was also a new hotel built in the shape of a boat, with a swimming pool and a small open air theatre with tiers of seats for spectators. Much of the village was covered with yellow and green paint and tiles to match the plastic seats. Even the above-ground gas pipes were painted in these two colours instead of the plain yellow found in the rest of the country. The reason they had above-ground gas pipes was that for some years after the collapse of the USSR, they did not have any gas, since Russia started charging them the full price for their gas instead of the minimal price they had been accustomed to. By the time they discovered they really did need gas, the underground pipes had decayed, and they felt it would cost too much to bury the new pipes underground, so they reverted to the highly dangerous-looking overhead pipes. I had seen these before in Uzbekistan, Georgia, and Armenia, always painted yellow.

Hotel in Vank.

Wall of Azeri car number plates, Vank.

The next day started fine, and we drove along poor (though better surfaced than the previous day's) roads to what once must have been a very large fortress at Mayraberd. Little remained but a few outer walls. This was connected by a wall to another castle on the other side of the river and protected the country from attacks by the hordes from the huge plain stretching six hundred kilometres to the Caspian Sea.

We then travelled on to the medieval fortress of Tigranakert, sitting on the ruins of the city founded by Tigran in the first century BC. Some of the ruins ran up a very steep hillside, and other bits were on the edge of a plain. Excavations were ongoing and included the foundations of a fifth-century church, proving, said George, that Armenian Christians were here long before Azerbaijan, which was only established in 1920, had even been thought of. The small fairy tale-looking castle now housed an Archaeological Museum, full of nesting swallows, which held many of the finds dating from the fifth to the seventeenth centuries, as well as a small café, where we had coffee. There were good views out over the plain on one side and up to the mountains on the other sides. Outside the castle, there was a stream and a deserted building, which had once housed a freshwater fountain. I gathered there were plans afoot to re-establish this as well as making a garden and a restaurant.

Our next visit was to the nearby deserted Azerbaijani city of Aghdam, which had been destroyed by the Karabagh army in 1994 to prevent it being recaptured by the Azeris, and it had subsequently been plundered for its stone by the local inhabitants. The only building that had not been destroyed was the mosque, whose minarets could still be seen from a distance. We were lucky to see the city, for some Karabagh soldiers had a camp there and often forbade entry to sightseers; however, we drove past their camp, and they did not interfere with us (though we only stopped for me to take photographs when we were out of their sight). We did not drive up the muddy track to the mosque, for we did not want to risk our luck.

During our visit here, the sky had clouded over, and just after we returned to the hotel, it started pouring, so we did not venture out for lunch.

Tigranakert Castle.

Minarets in destroyed Aghdam city.

After lunch, the rain stopped, so I took another walk round the city. At one point, I was stopped by a man who spoke no English but pointed to me and said, "England?" When I said I was, he smiled broadly and said, "England 1" and held up one of his fingers, adding,

"Ukraine 0." He made a sign showing a nought with his finger and thumb. He assumed I would understand this was the result in the latest World Cup football match. Since the weather remained dry, George took me to another open air restaurant on the edge of the city, for another excellent supper.

The next morning was unusual, to say the least. When we departed from the hotel, the whole place was swarming with police, possibly due to the arrival of the president, whose procession en route we had seen the previous day. Luckily, we were not delayed and drove some thirty kilometres to see a tree: this was a platanus tree, which had been acclaimed as the oldest tree (over two thousand years old) in the old Soviet Union. The road was uneven in quality, but parts of it had been donated by a rich Armenian woman and were better than the rest.

When we arrived at the track leading up a steep hill to the tree, we found the hut where George had been intending to pick up a truck to take us up was shut, so he drove farther down the road to find transport. There was no way he could drive his own vehicle, and he said that the agent's statement that it was an "easy" walk of three kilometres (it implied return) was absolute rubbish. He had once done it as a young man, and it had taken him almost two hours of abominable walking. He eventually found a man to drive us up in an incredibly ancient rusty Lada with a cracked windscreen and 454,448 kilometres on the clock. After checking the fuel level (with a stick picked up off the ground), he poured a little more petrol in from a dirty plastic bucket. On his fourth attempt, he managed to start the engine, and the car, coughing badly, set off up the worst track I had ever seen, suitable only for a tractor. Somehow he did not get stuck in any of the very deep muddy ruts or scrape his rusty exhaust off the car, and eventually we reached the tree, which still had a rusty board dating from the Soviet times, describing the tree in several languages. Although the tree was hollow, it seemed remarkably healthy, and someone had lit votive candles inside. There were large piles of stones scattered around; the intention was to lay an even stone platform and tidy up the whole area and make it a tourist attraction. I must admit I cannot see this happening in the near future, and certainly it will need to have far better access than it has at the present. Since Karabagh is not able even afford to keep its main roads in a reasonable state, I do not see the authorities spending a large sum of money to turn the so-called track into something reasonable for an ordinary car.

Two-thousand-year-old platanus tree.   Aged Lada transport.

On our return down, we gave a lift to two peasant ladies, who were travelling to Shushi. Their Armenian accent was such that even George could only understand one word in four. After we dropped them, we drove back over the frontier, very quickly this time, for George handed the official a sheet of paper from the foreign office to say I had a visa; the man did not even bother to look at it, since he was busy speaking to a friend. We stopped at the hotel in Goris for lunch and then drove the fairly short distance to Sisian, described by George as "the coldest and poorest town in Armenia". We were to stay at the hotel on the main square, which had not changed its appearance since it had been left by the Soviets (though there were some amusing statues of lions and fountains which were not functioning). The hotel was very basic, with a peculiar and terrifying shower apparatus, but clean. I spent much of the late afternoon touring the town and found there was some new building happening across the river as well as a number of further modern statues of citizens and local events. The museum was closed but had attractive roses and exhibits of grave carvings in the garden.

Lion statue in Sisian town square.

Outside Sisian museum.

When I returned to the hotel, I found it completely dark inside, due to a power cut, making climbing the stairs tricky. Luckily, half an hour later, power was restored and George and I were able to have a pleasant supper in the otherwise completely empty dining room in the hotel.

When I drew the curtains next morning, it was cloudy, but by the time I had finished the very sparse breakfast, the sky had cleared, and it remained sunny for the rest of the day (though we heard a lot of distant thunder while we were at Lake Sevan). We started by driving the few miles to see Karahunj, which was the Armenian equivalent of Stonehenge. It was in lovely countryside overlooked by mountains and, unlike Stonehenge, was not overrun by visitors. Indeed, we were the only visitors there except for a lone dog, who was howling in a disturbing manner until he heard an answering bark from some distance away and immediately trotted off, quite happily, in that direction. This monument contained over two hundred rough-hewn basalt stones arranged in a way suggesting an ancient astronomical observatory. Many of the stones had a hole carved through the top, for some unknown reason. It dated from about 2,000 BC.

Karahunj, the Armenian Stonehenge.

We next had a wonderful drive over a pass of 2,237 metres with a distant brief view of Ararat, before descending some 1,500 metres to the level of Yerevan and then turning up into the mountains again, only stopping to see a caravanserai dating from 1320 at a height of 2,300 metres. This building stood in a striking position with a lovely view and had some interesting carvings on the front; it was in excellent condition.

Armenian mountain caravanserai.

We then drove over another pass some 2,500 metres high before descending to Lake Sevan, where we stopped at Noratus to see the wonderful Field of Khachkars, a cemetery with some 900 of these marvellous monuments, no two alike.

Field of Khachkars Cemetery, Noratus, Lake Sevan.

We travelled on to the Sevan Peninsular, where we had lunch in a crowded restaurant with fine views over the lake, from where we could see thunderclouds gathering over where we had been on the other side. One of the tour groups there was being led by one of George's colleagues. The level of the lake itself dropped considerably during the Soviet occupation, since it had been used as a huge reservoir, and more water was being taken out than the rains and rivers were putting in. This had changed after Armenia gained its independence; water levels were gradually rising, and there was now the possibility that the peninsular will once again become an island; several houses had to be abandoned already.

There were several notices warning that there were 220 steep steps to reach the two churches. Undeterred, I climbed up to see the churches, one of them with a marvellous khachkar, before continuing on up many more steps and an uphill path to reach the top of the peninsular, with lovely views over the lake and up into the mountains.

Lake Sevan.   *Khachkar in Lake Sevan church.*

Few people had attempted the first lot of steps, but one of the few turned out to be an American Armenian I had met on the plane out and who was here for a wedding. It was interesting that I met quite a number of American Armenians who had come over to visit the country of their origins. The number of British visiting appeared to be very limited, though I did meet one small tour being led by another of George's colleagues.

We next drove farther along the lake edge, passing on the way the awful hotel that Jacynth and I had spent one night in on our only visit to the area. It looked even more derelict than it had on that previous visit, and I would not be surprised if it was soon invaded by the rising waters. The hotel we stopped at proved to be a fine new building, with a separate dining room some hundred yards away; it was by the lake side but well above the water level.

We were very lucky with the weather the next day, for it started sunny, and all our visits were made in fine weather (though thunderstorms affected the neighbouring mountains). Only a few drops hit the café in which we were lunching, and another storm hit while we were having supper in our hotel in the evening. We started with a long drive through the mountains to Haghartsin Monastery. Haghartsin itself had changed greatly since my previous visit. Then it had been deserted except for a French-speaking priest who showed us around. Now it was crowded with visitors, and many of the buildings, such as the refectory, had been reconstructed (not always successfully, and it had lost much of its original charm, though its woodland setting still remained). I was glad that the large 700-year-old walnut tree had survived, for quite a number of the roots on one side had had to be cut through because they were damaging the foundations of the Church of the Mother of God. Luckily, the roots on the other side kept it healthy, though it was now hollow. Also, the original working oven in the bakery was still there. The priest on our previous visit had proudly told us that this was still used, though whether it still was now, I could not find out. There was also a new seminary being built just nearby.

Haghartsin Monastery. *Khachkars, Haghartsin.*

We next travelled to the collection of buildings making up Goshavank Monastery, giving a lift to a soldier for part of the way. There were a fair number of visitors here, though nothing like as many as at Haghartsin. There had at one time been a university here. It also had a famous library, whose 1,600 books were burnt by the Mongols in 1375. The little chapel where Gosh, who had founded the monastery was buried was still visible some way up the hillside. There was some fine carving above a doorway as well as an excellent khachkar to be seen. Altogether, it had kept its ethos more than Haghartsin.

Goshavank Monastery.

We drove on to Dilijan, where we had lunch in a restaurant in a restored area of the little town. This street had been restored by rebuilding the houses in traditional nineteenth-century Armenian style, and there was also a small and attractive museum of artefacts from that period, as well as an attractive little craft shop where locals sold their wares. I went in and bought a silk painting for a ridiculously cheap price. When I returned home, it cost me three times as much to have it framed. When we left this attractive street, we went to a guest house, since the hotel we had originally booked had for some reason been closed. This was not a disaster, for I found myself with a large private lounge and a balcony, and my private bathroom was only a few steps down the corridor. One of the armchairs in my lounge was occupied by the largest teddy bear I had ever seen. While we were eating our excellent supper, George had a call on his mobile to say that, not long after we had left, Goshavank had been hit by a tremendous thunder and hailstorm, which had damaged many trees.

I was pleased to find it dry the next day, and as we journeyed up through lovely country to Sanahin Monastery, the sun broke through. After driving through a mile and a half tunnel, we emerged to find that what had been a land of treeless mountains had changed to a heavily wooded valley, which led us downhill to Vanadzor, a depressing town, for all the factories had closed with the collapse of the USSR, leaving empty ruins and an unemployment rate of over 40 percent. However, a drive along the river valley brought us to the far more attractive town of Alaverdi, set in a deep valley almost on the frontier with Georgia (in fact, only ninety kilometres from Tbilisi). Here, we saw a cable car leading up to the village of Sanahin, which had a large factory as well as the monastery. We did not take the cable car but drove up a very steep windy road; I was not surprised to learn that most of the factory workers who lived in Alaverdi used the cable car to get to work. I was interested to find that, what on my previous visit had been an empty flight of steps up to the monastery, was now lined with stalls selling religious artefacts. This may have been because it was a Sunday and more people would have been there than usual, though most of them had left by now, as the service was over. Indeed, the main church was shut and locked, and George had to find a caretaker to open it for us. She said she had to lock it these days because parents of young children no longer taught their offspring how to behave in a church. It was true that several small children were charging around, but in the main, I did not see any reprehensible behaviour. I had the feeling she was slightly over-reacting.

Sanahin Monastery.

This monastery was built of dark grey stone and was said to be the oldest in the country. The Church of the Redeemer, built in the second half of the tenth century, was the most dominant of the several buildings, and there was a fine view of the mountains on the other side of the Alaverdi Valley. The place was obviously very active, but quite a lot of restoration needed to be done, for grass and weeds were growing on the roofs, and the outside graveyard needed some tender loving care. The main gavit was very much larger than the actual church to which it was attached, and it contained several interesting grave stones. There was also a carving on the outside of the building of the two brothers who had built the monastery, presenting it to God. This was quite a common thing to find on Armenian churches. There was another of the same pair of brothers on the Hagpat Monastery, which we were to visit after lunch in Alaverdi.

Sanahin Monastery.

Hagpat was reached after another drive up a long and very steep hill. I remembered this as one of my favourite places from my previous visit to Armenia. Like Sanahin, it was made up of a cluster of buildings; one room that used to be a library had storage jars from the nineteenth century, when it was used for other purposes.

Hagpat Monastery.

The monastery also contained what I was told was the only khachkar in Armenia with a crucifixion scene on it. A little way outside the walls, there was a fountain building of similar age to the main monastery which had water running down through a series of basins, starting with one for pilgrims to drink from and then leading down through ones for bathing, for washing clothes, and for animals.

Road to fountain, Hagpat.   *Hagpat Monastery and khachkar.*

Our tiny hotel of twelve rooms was down a lane some way below the monastery, and it had lovely mountain views. Despite its small size, it had a little swimming pool with washing hanging out by it, so that I wondered whether it had been used for other purposes than swimming. The rooms were absolutely spotless, though once again I did not dare to use the shower plumbing, especially as there was no tray to catch the water. Apparently even George failed to get the shower to work. The meal taken in the little open air restaurant in the warm evening sunshine was excellent.

The drive back to Yerevan in bright sunlight was lovely, though clouds over Mount Ararat denied us excellent views of that mountain. We drove through several tunnels to Spitak, which had been the epicentre of the 1988 earthquake and was almost completely destroyed, but it was now rebuilt and thriving. Later on, we turned off onto a minor road to the Fortress of Amberd, and immediately after the junction, we stopped to visit a remarkable sculpture park in which each of the exhibits was a huge letter of the Armenian alphabet. Here we met a coach load of Canadian Armenians, including a professional photographer who took several pictures of me. Unfortunately, I was not able to email him and so have not seen the results.

Several miles farther along the road, we reached the Fortress of Amberd, which was a popular day outing from Yerevan. I could see why, for it was one of the most beautiful places I had ever visited.

Alphabet Park.

Amberd Castle.

Amberd Church.

The castle, with the small church below it, stood on a ridge where two gorges joined. The whole area was completely clothed in wild flowers. Before I went down to see the church, George told me not to try to climb back too quickly; the church was at a height of 2,300 metres, and many people, not realising the rarity of the air at that height, completely exhausted themselves climbing back. Luckily I managed, without too much trouble, to climb up again to the open air café, where we had a pleasant lunch before returning to Yerevan. The temperature rose rapidly as we descended from Amberd. It was 18 degrees Celsius at Amberd and 32 degrees Celsius down at the 1,000-metre height of Yerevan.

There was a sudden torrential rainstorm about ten minutes after we reached the hotel, but it only lasted for a quarter of an hour, so that I was able to take a good walk in bright sun before having another excellent meal at an open air restaurant.

In the morning, we went to visit three places near Yerevan. My itinerary said this was included, but I was told then that it had to be paid for. I agreed to do this provided I had a receipt, which I presented to Regent on my return home and was given an immediate refund and an apology. We first went to the church of St Hripsime. The church, dating from 618, was built over the mausoleum of this female saint, which had been constructed in 395. Her present tomb appeared to be modern.

St Hripsime Church, Ejmiatsin.

Tomb of St Hripsime.

Ejmiatsin, the spiritual centre for Armenian Christians, was only a short distance away. The cathedral was originally built on the site of an old pagan temple, and on my previous visit, a door was unlocked so that Jacynth and I could visit the underground room in which the first Christian altar was built in the old pagan temple. We had been very lucky, for I gather that nowadays entry to this very ancient holy site was strictly forbidden. The whole area around the cathedral had recently been restored; indeed, work was still continuing. The entrance was now through a fine modern arch, and there was a magnificent modern khachkar. The cathedral itself was completely renovated in the seventeenth century. The frescos inside, dating from 1720, were removed in 1891 but restored in 1956.

Entrance to Ejmiatsin.

Ejmiatsin Cathedral.

Modern khachkar, Ejmiatsin.

There were quite a number of visitors, but not nearly as many as I had seen in most of the Georgian churches I had been to the previous year. We were unfortunately not able to visit the museum, since it was locked and the curator would not be available for a couple of hours.

We turned off the main road on our way back to Yerevan to visit the ruins of Zvartnots Cathedral. This was built in the middle of the seventh century and, to judge by what one can see, was intended to surpass even Ejmiatsin in size. However, it was destroyed in an earthquake in 930 and was eventually completely covered by earth; it was only rediscovered in the first part of the twentieth century. Some restoration had been done and other stones were laid out in a way that suggested more may be carried out later. Unfortunately, what should have been a good view of Mount Ararat was once again obscured by the heat haze.

Zvartnots Cathedral near Ejmiatsin.

After our return to Yerevan, I decided to visit the National Gallery in Republic Square. My guide book noted that the pictures were only labelled in Armenian, but this had changed, and a worker was busy taking down the old labels and replacing them with ones in three languages, including English, so I was able to discover who many of the artists were and how they had named their subjects.

I had an early, and excellent, supper in the restaurant I had visited on my first day, and then I retired to bed in order to rise shortly after midnight to catch my early morning flight home.

I was glad to have taken this trip when I did, for a recent article in the *Times* speculated about the real possibility of a new war between Armenia and Azerbaijan.

Zvartnots Cathedral near Ejmiatsin.

Gavit in Hagpat Monastery.

CHAPTER 12

ISTANBUL AND CENTRAL ANATOLIA

Alahan Monastery.

My final trip of 2012 was to be to Turkey again. This time I was to spend three nights in Istanbul before flying to Ankara. The flight out was made more interesting for me, because by chance Rufus Reade, head of a holiday firm, was leading one of his tours out, so I was able to meet him in person (I had spoken to him on the phone several times). The visa queue at Istanbul Airport was much quicker than on previous visits, and the passport queue, though huge, moved more speedily, so that I arrived at the luggage hall long before the luggage. Indeed, the driver who met me said it had only taken ninety minutes from landing until I appeared.

The traffic in Istanbul itself was worse than ever, despite the short cuts my driver attempted along back streets. During the course of the journey, his boss rang up to speak to me and arrange the time to pick me up for my next flight. She told me she remembered picking me up herself two years previously, when she took me to the Avicenna.

I had an excellent evening meal at the hotel rooftop restaurant. The next morning, I was very amused to read a notice in the open air breakfast area which said, "Please do not feed the cats. They do not belong to hotel". It reminded me of the time three years before when I had been there with my daughter and grandchildren and a cat, carrying its baby in its mouth, had run through at speed and made a great leap up to the top of the wall before disappearing.

This proved to be a lovely sunny day, not too hot, and since it was a Sunday, I decided to go to the English service in the church near the Galata tower on the other side of the Golden Horn. There was now a complicated machine to obtain tokens for the tram, but a kindly Turk showed me how to work it and then came running after me with the one-lira coin I had left in the machine. Since I was early, I had a good walk in the street, largely pedestrianised except for the old-fashioned tram and police cars, and I also saw the famous Pera Palace Hotel, which I had stayed in many years before. It was recently modernised, but I was pleased to hear it had retained its wonderful Victorian lift (though I was horrified by the monstrous tower block which had been built just opposite it).

In the church service, I again met an English couple we had met there three years before; they lived not far from Elinor and my grandchildren and had become friends of theirs. After the service, which was enjoyable despite a sermon lasting forty minutes, I went and saw the Tekke of the Whirling Dervishes, which had been turned into a Dervish museum. They still gave occasional performances there for the tourists, but I fear this had lost the magic of the first time I saw them, when it was still a religious service.

After returning by means of the Tünel railway, I walked across the Galata Bridge to the Spice Bazaar, where I was offered Turkish Viagra, an offer I firmly refused. I then took the tram back to near Sultan Ahmet and visited the Pudding Shop for lunch. This was the first café in Istanbul we had visited back in 1973, and I had made a habit of re-visiting it; it had developed from a backpackers' resort to a popular tourist eatery. On one of my visits, I had been given a Pudding Shop tee shirt as a present, and on this occasion I was wearing it. When this was spotted, I was summoned to meet the manager and given two postcards and a car sticker.

I had two main objectives for this visit to Istanbul. The first was to once again see St Sophia, one of my favourite buildings in the world. I was startled to see a queue a hundred metres long to enter, but when the policeman on duty saw me, an elderly man with a stick, he waved me straight through and sent me to a separate part of the ticket office, where there was no queue at all. There are some advantages in being old.

I was delighted to find that there was no scaffolding at all inside the building, so for the first time since my 1973 visit, I was once again able to have a full uncluttered view of the marvellous space.

Interior of St Sophia, Istanbul.

I was also helped since my new camera proved to be very good in low light situations, without any need for flash, which was especially important for the photography of the mosaics when no flash was allowed.

My other reason for wishing to see Istanbul again was to visit the Suleymaniye Mosque, which had been closed for restoration on each of my previous two visits. This time I was lucky, though the magnificent turbes were closed on this occasion for their restoration.

Mosaic of St John the Baptist, in St Sophia.   *Restored Suleymaniye Mosque, Istanbul.*

The next day, I was picked up in good time for me to catch my flight to Ankara, where we arrived early; I was actually in the entrance hall with my luggage some time before we were even scheduled to land, so I was not unduly worried that my driver was not there to meet me. However, when he had not arrived after I had been waiting for the better part of an hour, I gave up and obtained a taxi to take me to my hotel, which proved to be on the other side of the city. When I arrived, I phoned my emergency number and was told my driver was waiting for me at the airport. Erkal, as he was called, finally turned up at the hotel at supper time; I found he had waited for two hours at the airport before his office had contacted him. It proved to have all been the fault of the office who had given him the time of my arrival in Istanbul instead of Ankara, and he had arrived some time after I had left but before the time he had been given. He came with his brother-in-law, who lived in Ankara, not far from my hotel, with whom he and his wife and daughter were staying for a family wedding, which he himself would not be able to attend because of driving me away from Ankara on the day of the wedding. The local agents made it up to me for the mishap by arranging for me to have my two evening meals free at the hotel instead of just breakfasts, which covered the cost of my taxi and was most convenient, for there were no nearby restaurant in this beautifully quiet suburb.

The next morning, we gave a lift to Erkal's wife as we drove into the city, since she wanted to do some shopping there. Our first visit was to the Museum of Anatolian Civilizations up on the Citadel Hill. We did not find it easy to reach since the usual road was closed, and there were no other signs showing the way. However, we eventually managed to reach it and parked nearby. I could hardly believe it when I saw there were notices apologising for disruptions caused by its own restoration. Luckily, it still had several rooms open, and all the most important exhibits were on show. I was particularly glad to see these, since this was my main reason for wanting to come to Ankara.

The Museum of Anatolian Civilizations, Ankara.

I had also hoped to see the citadel itself as well as a nearby mosque, but both of these were closed for restoration, so we drove on to look at some of the few Roman remains left in Ankara. The Roman baths, which I had seen on a previous visit, were not very impressive, so I was not too sorry that they proved to be shut. The Column of Julian was quite impressive, though no longer standing on its original site. For some peculiar reason, it is often called the Queen of Sheba Minaret. The main monument left was the Temple of Augustus. Erkal was a little surprised that I decided to walk up the hill to this, instead of taking the car from where he had parked. However, he soon became used to the fact that, despite my age, I was still active on my feet. The temple itself was not particularly impressive; its main importance was due to an inscription written on it. It had undergone several changes of use during its life, first to a church and then to a Muslim medressa before reverting to an historical remain. Very recently, an attractive garden was built round it.

The Temple of Augustus, Ankara.　　　　　　*The Column of Julian, Ankara.*

We next drove through the dreadful traffic to the very different Mausoleum of Ataturk. I found this building surprisingly impressive. A large part of the inside had been converted to a modern museum, showing Ataturk's campaigns in a way that may well not be to everyone's taste, but which would certainly have been enjoyed by the young, with its battle sound effects and Madam Tussaud-type figures. Photography was not allowed, so I resisted the temptation to take a picture of a middle-aged Turkish lady in national dress, standing immediately under a large notice saying "No Photography" in several languages, photographing one of the battle scenes. Outside, the mausoleum had not changed much, and I once again surprised Erkal by walking down the long Lion Avenue to see the statues of the stylised Turkish men and women at the far end. I was also lucky enough to witness the changing of the guard, even though I do not like their goose-step style of marching.

Ataturk's Mausoleum, Ankara.　Turkish men, Lion Avenue.　　Lion Avenue, Ataturk's Mausoleum.

When I was leaving the breakfast room the next morning, two waiters came up to me and asked me, very politely, if I would mind telling them how old I was. Since I have found the Turks frequently want to know everything about their visitors, I was quite happy to reply that I was eighty-three. Their jaws dropped, and I discovered they had thought I was in my sixties, Then the older of the two seized my left hand and pulled it, backside uppermost, towards him and solemnly bent over it and kissed it. I had never before had this reaction.

Whether it was the shock of this, or the result of advancing age, when I took my case down to the car, I inadvertently left the better of my two cameras on my bed. I did not discover the fact until we were down in the maelstrom of the Ankara traffic. Erkal, very sensibly, immediately found somewhere to park, phoned the hotel, and arranged for it to be sent down to us by a taxi, which proved to be a very great time saver.

Once we had left the city, we found ourselves on a nearly empty dual carriageway leading us towards our destination: the chief Hittite area. For most of the way, we drove through bleak treeless country, but this changed to an area of many more trees, especially poplars, which are very popular in Turkey. After a stop for lunch at a very basic-looking café, but which served us pizzas which were far better than anything I have ever had in England (where I only eat pizzas in emergency), we drove on to the site of Alacahoyuk. This was rather out of the way, and on my previous visit, the only thing to be seen was a particularly fine gateway in the middle of a stretch of wall covered by Hittite carvings. Since then, the archaeologists had been very busy; indeed, there was a group of about ten of them at work digging when we arrived. The site was far larger than I had imagined; many tombs had been uncovered and were now on display under glass, with their contents (or probably replicas of their contents) on display in their original positions. What was of particular interest was the number of animal skulls found in the tombs. The site had also sprouted a small museum to show the finds, which included several fine "Hittite teapots", according to the English translation on their labels, dating from 1,600 BC. Of visitors, we only saw a group of three, so it was not yet on the normal tourist route, although it was now a site of considerable size.

Hittite remains at Alacahoyuk.

Our next stop was at Yasilkaya, near to the main site of Hattusas. According to my guide book, in 1976, a French archaeologist removed some of the centuries-old patina which had protected the rock carvings from the elements, with the result that they were steadily losing their clarity. Certainly some of the carvings were decidedly less clear than I remember from my last visit. There were some archaeologists at work this time, climbing up some of the rock faces on the most rickety looking home-made ladders I had ever seen. I would not dream of climbing up them for more than a couple of rungs. I hope the present workers were able to arrest the deterioration. The entrance to the sanctuary of the small site was through a narrow crack in the rocks, and the carvings there were more protected from the elements and in better condition. Once again, as at Alacahoyuk, there were few other visitors.

Hittite site at Yasilkaya.

The great Hittite site of Hattusas was on a very different scale, with defensive walls 6.4 kilometres long with some two hundred towers. Inside the entrance there was a tarmac road, so one was able to drive round just inside the remains of the city walls. One small section near the entrance was a modern reconstruction of the walls to show what they would have been like before falling into the present low-level ruins, or in some parts foundations. The best preserved were at the highest level of the steep hilly area on which the city had been built, and it was from the top here that it was possible to get a good view over the whole city and see what a remarkable place it must have been.

We first stopped at the Great Temple, from where we saw across to the village of Bogazkale and the section of reconstructed wall. Inside, there was a large water basin carved from a single piece of limestone. But even more remarkable was a huge polished green marble stone, standing by itself in one of the temple rooms. Where it came from, and what its purpose was, was completely unknown. Our next stop was up on the hill at the Lion Gate, so called because of the carved lions on the entrance pillars.

Green marble stone, Hattusas.

Lion Gate, Hattusas.

At the highest point of the wall, at the Sphinx Gate, there was a tunnel about seventy metres long, running right through to the outside, from where one could see a section of the cyclopean wall, which was angled to fit into the hillside. This time, we did what I had not done before and followed the wall for some way till we came to a wide, steep, and very worn stairway, which led up a considerable distance to the top of the wall. While we were scrambling up the stairs, Erkal (who was behind me) took a very unflattering photo of me scrambling up: almost, but not quite, on my hands and knees. We then walked back along the top of the wall, with its fine views over the whole ruins of the city, including the foundations of the buildings, where there were thousands of inscribed clay tablets, from which we have discovered much of what we know about the Hittites, to near the tunnel, where another rough stairway led us down to our starting point. Our next stop was at the King's Gate, where there was a copy of the carving (the original of which was now in the Ankara Museum) which was originally believed to be that of a Hittite king but was now believed to be that of a god. Through the gate, a Turkish family of four was having a picnic and asked us to join them, but we needed to get on and so politely refused.

Entrance to tunnel, Hattusas.

King's Gate, Hattusas.

My pre-booked little hotel at Bogazkale, the village just outside Hattusas, was very basic, though clean. Erkal decided he would go and check out the other, slightly superior-looking hotel that we had seen in the village, but he soon returned and said that he too would stay in my place. He never told me why he had changed his mind, but I got the impression that the alternative had an interior that was definitely inferior. The evening meal, which we both took at the hotel, was excellent.

The next day, we started by visiting the little museum. The most interesting exhibits were two sphinxes, one of which had only been returned to the museum less than a year earlier, after having been sent to Berlin for repairs in 1917 and which had then resided in the Pergamum Museum. Long negotiations for its return had at last been successful. The rest of the exhibits were a mixture of objects found locally or copies of some now on exhibition in the Ankara Museum, with a few imitations of other Hittite objects.

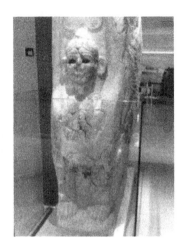

Bogazkale Museum, by Hattusas.

We then drove to Hacibektas, which was the fourteenth-century monastery of a branch of Dervishes founded by Haci Bektas, an order which was closely connected to the Janissaries and survived their extermination. They were very free thinking and even allowed unveiled women to take part in their ceremonies. Since 1926, it had been a museum but was still much venerated by the locals and was visited by them as a holy shrine. It was well out of the normal tourist route. Recently, the custom of tying prayer rags to the old mulberry tree had been stopped in an effort to save it from damage, but the spring with holy water was still used for drinking.

Hacibektas Monastery.   *Holy water spring, Hacibektas.*   *Ceiling of Tekke, Hacibektas.*

Our next stop was at Avanos, a town on the edge of Cappadocia, where we stopped for lunch at a crowded restaurant; Erkal lived not far away and met several old friends and managed to get us a private table on the edge of the river. After lunch, we had a walk round the town, where I was glad to see that the shop where Jacynth had bought her favourite sweater was still in existence, as was the place where we had seen some of the red clay pots being made. We then drove to see the Yellow Caravenserai which, though small, was remarkable for the colour of its stone. I had only seen its exterior before, since it was being restored, and so was pleased to be able to visit it properly. There were no other visitors there, for it was not on the normal tourist route either.

The Yellow Caravanserai, Cappadocia.

We next drove to the Zelve Valley, stopping on the way at a popular, and very crowded, view point for the Fairy Chimneys. To my surprise, Zelve was considerably less crowded than at the previous stop, possibly because exploring the valley and its cliff churches and pigeon lofts involved a considerable amount of walking and climbing. Erkal had obviously decided that I did not need continual looking after and remained at the entrance, chatting to some friends. I found the walk well worthwhile. At one point, a professional photographer from Istanbul insisted on taking my photograph many times. Maybe I will appear in some publicity material in the future!

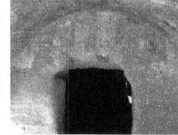

View point, Cappadocia.   *Churches in the Zelve Valley, Cappadocia.*

We stopped for tea at a café in Cavushin, below a cliff at the top of which someone was building a cave hotel. Since the only entrance appeared to be up a steep, narrow stairway on the edge of the cliff, with no guardrail or wall to protect anyone who slipped from falling down the sheer drop below, the view of the locals was that it was a doomed venture. Luckily, my cave hotel proved to be a very different matter. One could drive right up to the entrance, and then there was a very short level walk to the cave rooms. My room proved to be large and luxurious, with the largest bed I had ever slept in, and the bath proved to be a Jacuzzi. The water was hot and everything clean. The only drawback was the dining room; although it served excellent breakfasts, it did not serve other meals. However, the owners directed me to a restaurant only a quarter of an hour's walk away and told me that if I asked the people there to phone them when I had finished, they would bring a car to pick me up for my return (an offer I never took up). This restaurant, which had an outside terrace, served wonderful food, so I ate there three times. There was taped music playing quietly, and I was suddenly startled to hear two English Christmas carols being sung: "God Rest You Merry Gentleman" and "Good King Wenceslas". Sitting in a warm temperature of about 30 degrees Celsius in

September in a Muslim country listening to English Christmas carols was definitely one of my more unusual experiences.

The next morning, Erkal picked me up after breakfast and drove me first to Derinkuyu, a small town with an underground ancient city (which I did not visit on this occasion) and also two large Christian Greek Orthodox churches. Both of these were turned into mosques in the 1920s after the expulsion of the Greeks. They were locked, though one of them was still in use as a mosque, and I was able to take a photo of the interior through a keyhole, but the other seemed unused and derelict. We then drove on to the town of Nigde, where the Seljuk Alaeddin Mosque of 1223, up on the citadel, had a beautiful doorway. There was also nearby an attractive sixteen-sided turbe, with fine carvings. The cave monastery of Eski Gumus, with some lovely frescos, the main object of my visit to this area, was only a few miles away. We arrived to find it had just been shut and locked for lunch. However, Erkal not only persuaded the custodian that he only had to turn a key to let us in, he also persuaded him to let us have a share of his lunch. There were no other visitors around at the time (indeed, I have only once, in several visits, met a small group there), so I was able to spend an uninterrupted walk around, viewing the frescos at leisure.

Orthodox church, Derinkuyu.

Alaeddin Mosque, Nigde.

Fresco in Eski Gumus Monastery.

Our next visit was to the Soganli Valley, which involved an attractive drive through the mountains, though because of the heat haze, we could only just make out what should have been a lovely view of the 3,916-metre-high Mount Erciyes Dag, an extinct volcano which is snow-capped the whole year round and dominates the landscape.

I had expected to meet far more visitors in Soganli; however, it was still not on the normal tourist trail; there were no coaches at all and only a couple of other cars. It was an attractive place with a number of churches with frescos in good condition, though none of them as fine as those in Goreme or Eski Gumus. We drove up the valley road to its end, stopping on the way to visit a couple of painted cave churches. When we parked, I left Erkal in the car while I crossed the stream and walked back on the far side to see two of the more interesting churches: "the Hidden Church" and the three-storey "Church with a Beret" which, while not having any frescos, had the distinction of having the exterior carved out of the rock in the shape of Byzantine churches. After I returned to the car, we visited the village of Soganli, where some of the village ladies make a small income by selling dolls dressed in delightful native costumes. I bought one of these, which was being finished while I watched, for my niece Isabella.

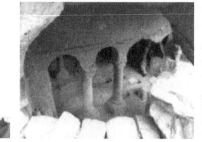

Soganli Valley, Cappadocia.

On our drive home, we stopped at yet another cave monastery which had recently been opened up. At my previous visit, many years before, only the church had been open, but now all the main buildings were visible, and there was even a little café in the grounds, where Erkal rested while I spent a considerable time exploring.

The next day, we started by visiting Ortahisar, an attractive little village, distinguished by a huge honeycombed rock cone fortress. This was where Erkal lived, and we actually saw his house. As in all Cappadocia, there were a number of stands with ceramic eyes for sale. These were supposed to be a guard against the evil eye.

Ortahisar, Cappadocia.   *Guards against the evil eye.*

Our main visit was to the Goreme open air museum. This I expected to be the most crowded place of my whole visit. We were lucky in the timing of our visit, for I did not have to queue for my entry ticket, and though there were a large number of visitors, it was not too busy for comfort. I spent three hours walking around here; Erkal had gone home for that time, and it proved to be the correct timing. This was I think undoubtedly the best area for these painted cave churches, though I was most disappointed to find that photography in the churches was no longer allowed, a rule which was strictly enforced. The Tokali Church, one of my favourites, was under restoration, and one was only allowed in for a short distance and so could get only a small impression of the magnificent frescos. However, "the Dark Church", which had been closed for ten years for restoration and safety work, was now open again, for an extra fee, and I decided the quality of its frescos was equal to those in the

Tokali. Despite the extra fee, there were quite a number of visitors. One small group was being quizzed by their Turkish guide as to the identity of some of the characters shown, and when none of them could answer, I fear I did so. As I was leaving the restaurant after supper that night, their guide, who happened to be feeding his group at the same place, recognised me and deserted his flock to come and speak with me for about quarter of an hour. Among other things, when I told him about my failure to get into the new Zeugma Museum the previous year, he told me he had had exactly the same experience when leading another group; although the firm for whom he worked was very large, the authorities had not thought to inform them of the delay in opening.

Several of the visitors to Goreme asked to have photographs of them taken with me; they said I looked distinguished, and one man from Ecuador said I was a marvellous example for my age, getting up so well to the higher places.

Cave churches in the Goreme Valley, Cappadocia.

We then moved on to Uchisar, with several photo stops and a visit to a large shop selling local jewellery and other artefacts, where I was given a glass of wine, even though I did not buy anything. Uchisar itself was probably the most visible place in the whole of Cappadocia because of its very tall fortress cone, from where it was possible to look out over a large part of this remarkable landscape.

Uchisar, Cappadocia.

It was another cloudless day when we left for Konya, and at one point the temperature reached 40 degrees Celsius, our hottest yet. When driving through Aksaray, I saw the café we had stopped at several times in the past; on our last visit, we had had the most disgusting ice cream I had ever tried in my life. Needless to say, none of us had eaten more than a mouthful then, and I did not suggest that we stop there this time. Instead we stopped, a little later, at Sultanhan, which I think was one of the finest of the old Ottoman caravanserai. Although this was still situated near the main road between Cappadocia and Konya, there were few other visitors, though we did meet a couple from our hotel in Goreme who were making for the south coast at Antalya. The sheer size of the covered area for the camels equalled that of many of our British cathedrals, whereas the mosque within the complex was comparatively small.

Sultanhan Caravanserai near Aksaray.

Konya, when we reached it, was to prove fairly full, not of foreign tourists, but of Turkish pilgrims to the Mevlana Tekke, the former home of the famous whirling dervishes and the tombs of Mevlana himself and other members of his family. The entrance had changed since my last visit, and there was now an attractive walk through gardens to the main building where, instead of removing our shoes, we covered them with plastic overshoes, which were then dropped into a rubbish skip when we left. There was less to see than I remembered from previous visits, and I later gathered that several displays, such as the early musical instruments used, were only put on show for special occasions, but it was still very impressive, and the taped music was the genuine thing from the religious services.

The Mevlana Tekke, Konya.

We next went to visit the Alaeddin Mosque on the hill in the centre of the city. This mosque, the burial place of eight Seljuk sultans, was closed for a long time for restoration and then for longer when it was discovered that the foundations were sinking in places and the whole building was in danger of collapse. All was now well, and the building, dating from the thirteenth century, with the prayer hall with over forty columns dating from many ages and topped with Roman and Byzantine capitals, as well as a beautifully tiled mihrab, was very well worth visiting.

Alaeddin Mosque, Konya.

Since it was a Monday, none of the other museums were open, so after I had been installed in my central hotel, I spent quite a long time walking round that area of the city. In the evening, I met an English couple in the hotel who knew a friend of mine in Sherborne.

As the museums were all open the next day, we spent the whole morning visiting them, which meant a lot of walking, since we left the car where we had managed to park it near the Karatay Medressa, now a tile museum, which had a lovely entrance doorway and a fine tiled dome inside. Several of the exhibit cases were empty, but my favourite Seljuk tiles, from a palace near Lake Beyshire, were still being displayed. The only other visitors were an elderly German couple. We then walked further round the central hill to the Ince Menare Medressa, with a fine tiled minaret and entrance doorway, with a display of wooden and stone, mainly Byzantine, artefacts. The only other visitors were the same Germans.

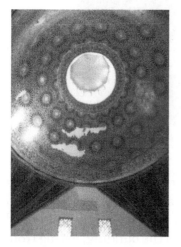

Karatay Medressa, Konya.

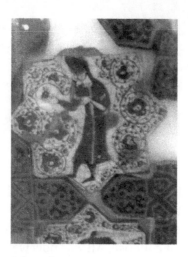

Seljuc tile, Konya.

Ince Menare Medressa, Konya.

We now had a considerable walk to the Archaeological Museum, which was hidden away in a maze of narrow streets. There was no one else at all visiting, despite there being an attractive display of small statues in the outside courtyard and as fine a display of sarcophagi as I have ever seen, as well as a number of artefacts from possibly the earliest city in the world ever discovered, Catal Huyuk, the site of which we were to visit the next day.

Displays in the Archaeological Museum, Konya.

Our last visit, a shorter walk away, was to the Ethnographic Museum. There were three staff on duty, but they still had to unlock it for us, since it was officially open, though there was no sign of any other visitors, and they locked it again when we left. This was, for me, the least interesting of our visits. We made our way back to the car by a more direct route, stopping at one point for a coffee break at a café by an attractive fountain.

In the afternoon, I walked down to the Mevlana Tekke to take some further photographs of the exterior. I then explored some more of the back streets, discovering among other things a modern Christian church and a large building labelled "The British Centre". I went into this to try and find out what it was, but inside the fine entrance hall, where there were two girls at their computers, I could find no one who could speak a word of English, which seemed odd for a British Centre decorated with large posters of London.

The visit to Catal Huyuk was taken on our way to Karaman and the Binbir Kilise (the Thousand and One Churches). Catal Huyuk was a little off the main road, so Erkal decided to approach it from the opposite direction to save having to retrace our steps at one point. His route proved to be considerably longer as it turned out, and at one point, we stopped and asked a couple of policemen the way, but they had never heard of it. Luckily, a few miles further on, we found a sign post pointing to it. I had gathered that there was not much to see, since the many artefacts had all been removed to other museums, and this proved to be the case. A party of three Germans were already there and watching the German version of the video about the site, and we had to wait and watch before the site guide would take us round. There were a few small objects and a number of faded photographs in the room, and outside was a small room which proved to be a reconstructed copy of one of the old houses. The excavated foundations of the site were under two huge roofed buildings, one of which had the shape of a vast woodlouse. They were obviously not weather proof, for many of the remains were covered by large white sandbags to protect them from the weather. We were told that excavations took place four months every year during the school summer holidays and that some of the older pupils helped. While I was glad to see it, I would certainly not take time out again for another visit.

Our main visit of the day was to the remarkable Binbir Kilise. This was visited by Gertrude Bell in 1905 and, to judge by her photographs, has not changed much since. There was now a narrow road with a proper surface, as opposed to the track of my previous visits. In the village in the valley below the mountain, there were the ruins of two very large churches.

Churches at Maden Sehir below Mount Karah Dagh, near Karaman.

However, the place of greatest interest was several miles farther on up Mount Karah Dagh. Here, there was a village made up of the scattered ruins of a great number of churches and monasteries. Experts say that some of these buildings dated from before the time of Constantine. Gertrude Bell said that some fifteen families had constructed themselves shanties out of the ruins. On my first visit, there were still about a dozen families living there, but now there were only four. Their dwellings were still very primitive, but electricity (and television) had arrived, and there were what looked like oil tanks in their gardens. The other buildings were now in ruins or used as barns or cattle sheds. One ruined church had at one stage been converted into a mosque, but it was now used for sheep. We were shown round by one apparently very old man (seven years younger than me), who had lived there all his life. We were the only visitors at this time.

Binbir Kilise (the Thousand and One Churches) on Mount Kara Dagh.

Karaman, where we spent the night, was a pleasant little town which reminded me very much of Malatya, where I had stayed the previous year. I had not stayed here before, but when driving through on a previous visit to Binbir, I was held up for a long time by a flock of geese marching steadily down the main dual carriageway in the middle of the town; they were not going to hurry up, or get out of the way of any traffic which also wished to use the road.

The next day, one of the few when there was a certain amount of cloud, we drove down to the south coast at Silifke, stopping on the way to visit the lovely ruin of the hillside church of Alahan. When we turned off the main road to drive the three-kilometre track up to the site, I was surprised to find it now had a covering of tarmac, though it was still as steep, narrow, and windy as before. When we reached the site, we found it was full of workmen restoring and making safe the various buildings. It looked as though there had been a rock fall in the very early cave church. This had now been made safe, and the workmen had established their headquarters in it. Work was going on at several other buildings, but we were able to walk along to the finest of the churches at the end. When we entered this church, the chief workman was giving instructions to two very young-looking girls, who were evidently new to the team. When they left, we had the place to ourselves. After we had returned along the path with its marvellous views, I asked Erkal what the large notice, in Turkish, at the entrance to the church had said. "Oh," he replied, "it said, 'Danger of collapse. Do not enter.'"

I only hope they do not try to "improve" what was a marvellous place.

Alahan off the road to Silifke.

We next drove on down to Silifke, a drive with the most wonderful views. The whole of that road was being turned into a dual carriageway, and unfortunately the fine view point down to the river (where Barbarossa was drowned during the Third Crusade and where there is a monument to him) was unreachable because of the road works.

After lunch at Silifke, we drove inland to see the remarkable Roman site of Dio Caesarea (or, to give it its modern name, Uzuncaburc), stopping on the way to see several remarkably well-preserved Roman tombs and temples. At the site itself, there was a small modern settlement, several of the houses being very primitive and obviously built mainly from stones taken from the ruins. There was actually one small coach load of visitors, with the coach parked right by some ancient columns, but it was otherwise empty, except for one young schoolgirl walking back to her home in the middle of the ruins. The site itself was large and included among its many remains the Temple of Zeus Olbius, which was the oldest known temple of the Corinthian order in the whole of Asia Minor and which became for a time a Byzantine-era Christian church; there were several other temples, a plethora of standing columns, and a five-storey Hellenistic tower about twenty-five metres high. At the moment, a fallen stone nearly blocked the entrance so that I was not able to get inside. A nearby village also contained the remains of a Roman aqueduct and a few Byzantine churches. I spent a couple of hours exploring, during most of which Erkal sat chatting with villagers in a local cafe. He had by now realised that he did not have to "nanny" me, and as he himself had visited before, he did not need to hunt around for new discoveries. We then drove down again to Silifke to look for our hotel, only to find that, despite the address we had been given, it was some ten miles farther east along the coast at a place called Korykos. Erkal was annoyed at this, since his father-in-law, who was away, had a house only a few miles farther on, and if he had known, he could have collected the key and stayed there for the next two nights.

Tomb near Dio Caesarea. Dio Caesarea, near Silifke.

I remembered Korykos itself as being a long beach with a delightful castle, known as "the Maiden Castle", on an islet out at sea, and a land castle at one end. Buildings were almost non-existent. Now it was a modern beach resort with many hotels. Our hotel was of over two hundred rooms and very much geared to tourists, with very little atmosphere. However, it was clean and comfortable with a good view of the Maiden Castle from the beach at the end of its garden. I also met the English couple, Dr and Mrs Liddell, that I had met at the Konya hotel. We shared a table for supper each of the two evenings we were there, and during the course of conversation, we discovered that we had many interests in common. They had also stayed at the ghastly hotel that I had stayed at the previous year in Batman. They too were travelling with Anatolian Sky but were luckier in that their driver was also an official guide. He worked for the same firm as Erkal, and they knew each other.

The next day was to be very full. We started by going to "Heaven and Hell". These were two steep chasms with caves at the bottom. One can only see Hell from a platform at the top of the 125-metre-deep pit, since the descent can only be taken with a guide if one is experienced in pot holing. The descent to Heaven was easier, being, according to the notice, 375 steps followed by a steep walk farther down to the ruins of a small second—or third-century church, outside the entry to the cave from where one could hear the roar of an underground river which the locals called the Stream of Paradise. I had been down on my previous visit, many years before, and so decided not to go down again, even though the church had apparently recently been restored. Some Roman and Byzantine ruins, including a high-walled basilica, were situated near the chasms.

Nearby was a cave which was sometimes called the Asthmatic cave, since it was supposed to help cure asthma. As I was told this was only ninety steps down, I decided to go and have a look. In fact, I counted them coming back up, and there were 145 steps, and quite a few steps up and down as well on the very uneven and slippery floor at the bottom. Nevertheless, I was very glad to have descended, for the stalactites and stalagmites were of the most marvellous colours, and though I had been in larger caves in the Mendips and in several foreign countries, this was in many ways the most remarkable of the lot. Erkal had originally remained at the entrance but was evidently told by the staff that the floor was very slippery and visitors sometimes fell, so he decided to come down and make sure I was not in danger. Luckily, no accidents befell either of us.

Our next stop was to see a tiny museum, once a Roman bath, down near the sea, where there was a remarkable mosaic of the Three Graces still in situ. Many years before, Jacynth and our friend Audrey had once stopped here for a cup of tea in a little café on stilts overlooking the sea. The tea was brewed in a Samovar and, to judge by its taste, had been brewing for some days. It was quite the worst cup of tea I had ever tasted. We did not stop this time.

Asthmatic Cave near Korykos.   *Mosaic of the Three Graces, near Korykos.*

We then travelled east, past Korykos, and stopped at Elaioussa, where excavations were still going on. Although this was right near the main road, there were no other visitors. It was not a large site but contained a good classical theatre and a very fine city gate as well as baths, a bit of an aqueduct, and other buildings.

Our visit, after lunch in a roadside café, was to be a few miles inland, just beyond the village of Kandlivane (meaning "the blood-stained place"), where there were the tremendous remains of ancient Kanytelis. This remarkable place had a chasm some sixty metres deep and ninety metres by seventy metres in area in the centre, which was supposed to have been where criminals were thrown down to be eaten by wild animals. On my previous visit, Jacynth and I had just driven to where we could see the city across the chasm, but time prevented us from stopping and exploring further. On this visit, I spent over two hours walking round, without seeing a single other person (for Erkal had remained in the car, reading a paper). How such a place can be so neglected when it was so near to several resorts, I cannot imagine, for in the UK, it would always be crowded. It contained the remains of a great number of houses, tombs, temples, and churches, and there was even a Muslim graveyard, which was obviously in use until very recently.

Elaioussa, near Korykos. Kanytelis, near Korykos.

After we returned to the hotel, I set out on foot to see the land castle at one end of the long beach. The walls of the building were very impressive, but when I had scrambled up a steep and very rough slope to gain entrance, I was met by a scene of desolation. It did not appear to have had anything at all done to restore it, and the ruins inside were covered with weeds and brambles. There were three rusty notice boards in Turkish and English, the first of which read "Obey the warning of guard". Needless to say, there was no guard (unless you counted the elderly lady at the ticket office, and she had said nothing at all). The second, which stood among some rubble, read "Save our historical monuments". The third, which stood among a pile of fallen stones and weeds, read "Keep neat our environment". Also, there were a few very narrow, rough, and uneven paths which were visible in places. I had to look very carefully wherever I went to avoid twisting my ankle or putting my foot into some deep hole.

When I left this castle, I again bumped into the Liddells, who persuaded me to join them on a trip to the Maiden Castle out in the sea. The small ferry only ran when the owners thought they had enough people on board, and we had to wait some time after boarding before leaving from the small jetty. The short journey was choppy, and when we reached the castle, we had to scramble out precariously onto large boulders since there was no jetty there. Once through the entrance gates, it was obvious much work was being done; a large section of the floor had been uncovered, showing tiles and some mosaics in situ. It was possible to climb the narrow, unprotected stairs up to the top of the walls in places, a very alarming proceeding. On returning, we had to wait some time for a boat to come and pick us up, and when one eventually arrived, we all helped each other to scramble aboard until there were many more than should have been allowed. However, we did get back safely, and no one fell into the sea. For almost the first time in my life, I found myself thinking kindly of our own health and safety brigade.

Korykos Castle.   *Maiden Castle.*

For our final day, we travelled past Adana to the little village of Missis. On my previous visit, we had seen a fine Roman bridge here. Unfortunately, this had been restored in an unfortunate manner, for it looked completely new, though keeping the shape of the old bridge. The main reason for our visit was to see the mosaic of Noah's Ark, which was displayed in situ in a modern building. We had difficulty in finding the building, since the sign posts to it were almost non-existent. However, we did eventually find the rough overgrown track which led to the little museum. To begin with, I was disappointed since the whole mosaic looked as though it had never even been dusted in the years since my previous visit. However, I was able to take photographs, and these emerged much more clearly than I had thought possible. There were a large number of animals and birds displayed, though nothing was shown to scale. The ark itself was shown like the Ark of the Covenant, with a bird's tail sticking out of it. I was able to send several photos to Dr Liddell, who asked if I would, since he had never seen it (and he often lectures on Noah's Ark).

We then went inland to the village of Anazarbus and its Roman site on the edge of a plain and at the foot of a mountain. This was obviously a very large settlement, though much of it remained to be excavated. There was a third-century triumphal arch still standing as well as the lengthy remains of the city wall, and one of the villagers discovered a couple of Roman mosaics in his garden, which he had turned into a tiny open air museum in which he also displayed several sarcophagi.

Noah's Ark Mosaic, Missis. Anazarbus.

We returned to Adana, where I booked into my hotel and took a walk to see the huge new mosque, which was one of very few outside Mecca with six minarets. Until recently, Sultan Ahmet (the Blue Mosque) was the only one. After a good night's sleep, I flew back via Istanbul, where the girl at the passport office expressed astonishment at my age when she saw the date of birth on my passport.

New mosque in Adana, with six minarets.

I am now looking forward to 2013 and have already booked trips to Burma and Kurdistan, and I am also planning a tour of Bulgaria. Time to start a new volume!

ADDENDA

I was recently looking through some old papers when I came across the following:

> "**February Talk.** These indomitable travellers, Dermot and Jacynth Hope-Simpson, have been at it again! This time Jacynth will talk to us about their recent adventures in **Syria with a side trip to Baalbec in Lebanon.** Never known to do things the easy way, they were stopped by the Hezbollah, complete with balaclavas and kalashnikovs, as they discovered some of the archaeological gems of this historic yet troubled region."

Despite this, we did not consider ourselves indomitable, and most of our travels were undertaken without any real scares. So here are a few of the things I have done when organising the trips in this book, which may give ideas to other elderly travellers:

1. **Planning.** I use everything I can get hold of, from guide books to the Internet, to find out as much as I can about the places I want to visit in a trip.

2. **Booking a trip.** I always book through a travel agent. Quite a few people I know book through the Internet as being cheaper, but several of them have encountered real problems when using this method. My local travel agents are very helpful in finding firms which can give me what I want. They, however, can only book through ABTA-recognised firms, so when I book direct with a non-ABTA firm, I make sure that it is bonded with ATOL. In this way, I know that I am covered if the firm goes broke. Even large firms have been known to do this, and there is seldom any warning given. Contrary to general belief, travel agent trips are *not* always more expensive than individually booked Internet trips, and you do have a safety net.

3. **Insurance.** This is more expensive for the elderly, but there are several firms which specialise in this market. It is well worthwhile shopping around, for differences in price can be considerable. I believe it is essential, for it is impossible to foresee what may happen.

4. **Cameras.** I have always taken two cameras with me since an early disaster. Digital cameras are so small and light, this is not difficult. Make sure your memory stick is large enough, and remember to take battery rechargers with you.

5. **Money.** Take advice from your agent about money where you are going. Remember that you are likely to get considerably worse rates of exchange at any airport. I always wear an under-clothing body belt for my cards and any excess cash. Even in hot climes, I wear a summer jacket with inside pockets. I often carry an empty (or almost empty) wallet in an outside pocket as a decoy. Once, in Barcelona, I had this taken.

6. **Medicines**. It is always worth taking a few basics such as tummy pills, pain killers, and elastoplasts. Also check with your GP that your travel jabs are up to date and whether you need anything else for the area to which you are travelling.

7. **The List.** I have a list of what I may want to take with me. I find this very useful to consult before I travel. If I don't use it, I nearly always forget something. It can always be added to if required.
8. **Books.** I always take something to read. Sometimes I never even open a book, but on other occasions, something readable is invaluable.

ABOUT THE AUTHOR

Dermot Hope-Simpson is a retired teacher and headmaster, who frequently travelled with his wife to places where few other tourists are to be found. He has a keen interest in history and archaeology. Since the death of his wife, a well-established children's author, he has continued travelling, sometimes going to even more unusual places. He has lectured to various societies and is a room guide at Montacute House, a large National Trust Elizabethan manor house.

He is also very active in church matters, serving on his Diocesan Synod, Diocesan Board of Education, and the Standing Committee of his Deanery Synod.

About the Book

After my wife died, I decided to remain active, including travelling. This book is an account of twelve journeys I made over the four years since then, and it is liberally illustrated with my photographs. Many of these journeys were individual but some were group tours. The places visited include various parts of Turkey, in particular the eastern part of that country. It also includes visits to Jordan, Albania, Uzbekistan, Warsaw, Iran, the former Russian Republic of Georgia, Kosovo, and Armenia with Nagorno Karabagh.

I am still travelling, and in 2013, I went to Myanmar (Burma), Bulgaria, and the semi-autonomous province of Iraqi Kurdistan. In the last of these, we were told we were the first tourist group ever to visit and as a result were greeted by the Minister of Tourism and the collected representatives of the local press and television networks.

Lightning Source UK Ltd.
Milton Keynes UK
UKOW06f1226190814

237172UK00002B/12/P